TALES FROM THE
ATLANTA BRAVES DUGOUT

TALES FROM THE
ATLANTA BRAVES DUGOUT

A COLLECTION OF THE GREATEST
BRAVES STORIES EVER TOLD

CORY McCARTNEY

SPORTS
PUBLISHING

Sports Publishing books may be purchased in bulk at special discounts for
sales promotion, corporate gifts, fund-raising, or educational purposes. Special
editions can also be created to specifications. For details, contact the Special
Sales Department, Sports Publishing, 307 West 36th Street, 11th Floor, New
York, NY 10018 or sportspubbooks@skyhorsepublishing.com.

Sports Publishing® is a registered trademark of Skyhorse Publishing, Inc.®,
a Delaware corporation.

Visit our website at www.sportspubbooks.com.

10 9 8 7 6 5 4

Library of Congress Cataloging-in-Publication Data is available on file.

Cover design by Tom Lau
Cover photo credit by AP Images

ISBN: 978-1-61321-900-3
Ebook ISBN: 978-1-61321-901-0

Printed in the United States of America

CONTENTS

Acknowledgments

Jimmy Carter taught Hank Aaron how to ski. It's true. The two were in Colorado in 1999 to celebrate Aaron's sixty-fifth birthday, these two members of American royalty, the thirty-ninth President of the United States and the Home Run King.

"I've been a close, personal friend of Hank since I first got to know him," Carter told me, some sixteen years after that excursion.

It was baseball that brought them together, two men who, at their cores, were a peanut farmer from Plains, Georgia (Carter) and a poor kid from Mobile, Alabama. They shared that passion as a fan and one of the greatest players in the game's history, respectively.

May the following stories spark that same love for the game, a love my father and grandfather—both named Karl—passed on to me.

This book is for the two of you, along with the young fans I'm taking to the ballpark for hot dogs and ice cream in mini helmets, my sons Jack and Cooper.

It's also for my incredible wife, Jama. If it weren't for your patience and understanding while this project consumed me, it wouldn't have been possible. It's for my mother, Deb, my brother, Tom, and brother-in-law, Kyle, my nephews, Alexander and Jamasen, and all those family and friends that suffered through me being holed up with my computer.

Thanks to Brad Hainje, Beth Marshall, Adrienne Midgley, and Chris Rice with the Braves; my friend Mark Lewis, along with Beth Davis and Lauren Gay for your work in securing an interview with Carter; Rachel Levitsky with the Major League Baseball Players Alumni Association; my boss at my day job, Jeff Genthner; my colleague and friend Zach Dillard; and, finally, my editor, Julie Ganz, for the opportunity and freedom to tell these tales.

"Baseball, it is said, is only a game," Pulitzer Prize–winner George Will once wrote. "True. And the Grand Canyon is only a hole in Arizona. Not all holes, or games, are created equal."

From that end, chronicling baseball comes with it a responsibility. I can only hope I've done baseball, and the people whose journeys I've chronicled, justice.

Something out of Heaven

A shuttle bus worked its way through the quaint streets of the quaint town that stands as baseball's Mayberry, while inside, a quiz of the utmost importance was being conducted.

"All right boys," said Tom Seaver, Mets legend. "Don't forget your wife's name. Seriously, practice it right now."

He turned to Bobby Cox, the former Braves manager, who in a matter of minutes, would be walking up to the podium to give his induction speech as a member of the 2014 Baseball Hall of Fame class.

For men used to operating under the gazes of tens of thousands of onlookers, pressure goes with the territory. But the very thought of forgetting to mention their significant other? That was terrifying.

"Now," Seaver said, "what's your wife's name?"

"Pam," Cox shot back.

"Don't forget it," Seaver replied.

He didn't.

Cox—whose twenty-nine-year managerial career saw him win five pennants and lead the Braves to fourteen straight division titles—thanked his wife and eight children "for their unwavering support, even though I spend half the year on the road and the other half at the ballpark" to close out his nine-minute, fifty-second speech.

To his right on the stage on the grounds of Cooperstown's Clark Sports Center sat two of the cornerstones of Atlanta's 1990s domination, pitchers Tom Glavine and Greg Maddux, themselves waiting for their turns.

Behind them all was a collection of fifty-five returning Hall of Famers, including Braves greats Hank Aaron and Phil Niekro. It was Aaron that received the longest ovation.

In the distance, in plain view of the stage, working as an analyst for MLB Network, was John Smoltz, another of Cox's Cy Young winners, who would receive his own HOF call a year later.

"It's like something out of heaven that landed here in Cooperstown," Cox said.

Heaven? No, more like Atlanta, as the day and the entire weekend belonged to the Braves.

"It represents what we were able to do in terms of turning the organization around and having the success that we had in raising this organization to the standard that we did in the 1990s," said Glavine, "which is the standard most clubs wanted to adopt and tried to emulate."

An estimated crowd of 48,000—the third-largest ever and sixteen times the previous year's total—descended upon the New York burg on July 27, 2014, to see the Braves trio, along with slugger Frank Thomas and managers Tony La Russa and Joe Torre. Thomas, La Russa, and Torre only deepened the connections to the Braves and Georgia, as

Thomas is from Columbus, Georgia, Torre was a former Braves player and manager, and La Russa also played in Atlanta.

"I don't think you can write a script any better than that," Niekro said.

To be fair, Maddux didn't go into the Hall of Fame representing the Braves. Faced with picking Atlanta or the Cubs, who drafted him and with whom he won his first Cy Young Award, the right-hander chose neither. But with three straight Cy Youngs and ten postseason appearances, to many, he will always be a Brave.

As Maddux put it, "People ask me why my Hall of Fame plaque has no logo. I spent twelve years in Chicago, eleven in Atlanta, and both places are very special to me. Without experiences in both cities, I would not be standing here today."

Before the ceremony began, Leo Mazzone, the former Braves pitching coach and Cox's right-hand man during the franchise's 1990s heyday, was talking to one of Cox's daughters. Her dad was nervous, and Mazzone, like he had done for Atlanta pitchers so many times, played psychologist.

"I told her to text him a message that said 'We've been in a lot tougher jams than this one,'" Mazzone said.

An impromptu tomahawk chop and chant broke out as MLB Commissioner Bud Selig introduced Cox, and he would later admit his hands shook as he began his speech. The game's all-time leader in ejections eased the tension with a joke.

"A few years ago," Cox said, "I was sitting with Steve Stone, the broadcaster for the Chicago White Sox, at an Arizona Fall League game, and this guy comes up and says, "Steve, can I have your autograph?" He says, "Sure." He signs it, and he says, "Hey, you don't want Bobby's autograph?" That guy just stared at me, and he says, "Yeah, I know you. You're that guy from Atlanta who gets thrown out all the time, right?" I said, "Yeah, that's me, but [Tommy] Lasorda, if he hadn't quit so early in his career, he would've had the record that I've got now."

While former general manager and current team president John Schuerholz watched, he couldn't help but reflect. For Schuerholz, the architect of those 1990s monsters, here was the manager he worked so harmoniously with, alongside the biggest free-agent signing of his reign (Maddux), and Glavine, another key piece of the core he built around for more than a decade.

"You're proud to be a world champion," he said, "but when the organization is represented like this, the excellence that is reflected in these three guys for what they did in baseball, to be recognized all at one time—in our organization—buttons are popping off our shirts. That's how proud we are."

Bill Bartholomay couldn't help but think back to the beginning as he took it all in. The club's chairman of the board and chairman emeritus, he was the owner who moved the Braves from Milwaukee to Atlanta in 1966, overcoming controversy and numerous legal battles.

One hundred years after Reconstruction, America's game had come to the Southeast, and with it a superstar in Aaron. It was those early days that set the stage for this baseball time capsule, and Bartholomay, along for that entire ride, soaked it in.

"So when I sat in Cooperstown . . . in between little rainstorms and whatnot and heard the talks and did all that stuff, that's what I was reflecting on," he said. "The people involved, the great managers, the great pitchers.

"Never again will two 300-game winners from the same team be inducted at the same time . . . That's something to be proud of. Very proud of it, anybody who was associated with it, and I'm the lucky guy that was in an ownership position and chairmanship position all the way through, pretty much."

It was Maddux that led off the ceremony, and before "The Professor" had even mentioned the Braves, he managed to give a glimpse of his mischievous ways.

Maddux was an infamous practical jokester—former teammate David Wells called him "The Silent Scumbag," though with total affection—known for, among the more printable transgressions, lighting players' shoes on fire. As Chipper Jones would tell MLB.com, "He's one of the grossest guys I've ever been around in my life."

So it should come as no surprise that, when his speech touched on his brother, fifteen-year MLB vet Mike, Greg Maddux disclosed this nugget: "He even taught me a little bit about science. It has to do with a little methane and a lighter, and I still get a huge kick out of it today. That's funny, huh?"

He wasn't done, directing his attention to Smoltz when he summarized his time with the power pitcher and Glavine, ending with a dig that would resurface a year later at Smoltz's induction ceremony.

"The next seven years were spent winning division titles, watching the kids grow up," Maddux said, "and watching John Smoltz's hairline recede."

Maddux later revealed it was the first prepared speech he'd ever given, and as for the striped tie he wore, he said, "I re-used this. My daughter had a fraternity party back in January and it was still tied so I didn't have to re-tie it. Second time this year."

Known for his efficiency and wasting little time on the mound—he once threw a complete game on just seventy-six pitches—he needed just ten minutes to deliver his speech.

Glavine would clock in at seventeen minutes, twelve seconds. Known for his unwillingness to give in on the mound, he was unafraid of walking batters, figuring that eventually they'd swing at something they normally wouldn't if he lived on the edge of the strike zone.

He picked this moment to let it be known where that trait came from.

"People always ask me where I got my qualities from," the left-hander said. "My work ethic I got from my dad, and as much as my mom hates to hear it—Mom, I'm sorry—I got my stubbornness from you."

The trio of Braves marked just the second time in history that three members of the same team were being inducted together, joining famed Cubs double-play combination Joe Tinker, Johnny Evers, and Frank Chance in 1946. It was also just the ninth time teammates were going in together, the most recent being the Dodgers' Don Drysdale and Pee Wee Reese in '84.

"This wasn't just good luck that caused all this to happen," Schuerholz said. "This was good intentions, good plans, good efforts, good God-given ability, good aggressiveness, good commitment to their level of professionalism and each and every job they had, and it's imbued throughout this entire organization."

But as Glavine thinks back on that weekend, he doesn't focus on his own experiences.

For a franchise that can boast Aaron, and the likes of Warren Spahn, Eddie Mathews, and—thanks to its founding as the 1871 Boston Red Stockings—can call itself the oldest continuously playing team in North American sports, its finest era was just getting started in its parade of immortals.

"It was kind of, looking at it, the start of what we all think is going to be a pretty decent little run here of guys representing this organization getting into the Hall of Fame," Glavine said. "So, yeah, certainly with me, Bobby, and Greg last year and knowing that John is coming and Chipper's coming, that John Schuerholz should be coming."

Schuerholz could be part of the Class of 2017 and Jones is eligible for election a year later.

That group helped the Braves become the gold standard of any American sports organization at their apex, a year-in and year-out triumph that became as cliché as death and taxes.

For Bartholomay, it was the culmination of possibility.

He saw an untapped region of fans, potential TV gold—a prophetic thought that would be expanded by his successor as team owner, Ted Turner—and a chance to expand the sport's reach in a major organizing center for the civil rights movement.

When the Braves played their first game in Atlanta on April 12, 1966, they did so against the Pirates, putting the likes of Aaron, Mathews, Torre, Roberto Clemente, Willie Stargell, and Bill Mazeroski on display.

"Baseball, football, and other sports recognized that some of the sociological barriers that had been there should not stand," Bartholomay said. "Baseball was in a position to do something about that and the Braves were the ones that were in the position to make a move."

Aaron's crowning achievement—surpassing Babe Ruth as Home Run King—would follow, as did the transformative Worst-to-First season of 1991 and Atlanta's lone pro sports championship in '95.

The franchise knew success before it arrived in the South, winning a championship in Boston in 1892, then a World Series in 1914 and another in Milwaukee in 1957. But in Atlanta it became a brand.

It became "America's Team."

That nickname was a dash of grandiosity from Turner, but rang true thanks to the draw of TBS.

Former Braves catcher Gerald Laird was a testament to that. He grew up south of Los Angeles, but when he signed with the team in February 2013, he didn't hide his true fandom.

"This was my favorite team growing up as a kid," Laird said. "I grew up in Southern California, but every day, 4:05 p.m. Pacific Time, I remember going home to watch the Brave game. Mom would say, 'You can watch the Brave game if you do your homework.'"

Like many in his generation, he was rushing to see Glavine, Maddux, and Cox.

They helped shape a franchise, but they weren't alone. These are the men and the events that have defined the Atlanta Braves.

Chapter One

Hank Aaron's 715: A New King and His Court

"What's he like? What do I expect?" a lawyer friend asked former Braves public relations director Bob Hope as they drove to the southwest Atlanta home of Hank Aaron. The legendary slugger would be appearing in a mock *SportsCenter* segment for the bar mitzvah of the attorney's son.

The former Braves director of public relations, who was alongside Aaron during his pursuit of Babe Ruth's home run record, didn't need long to mull it over.

"First of all, you'll go in there and tell him, 'Hank, I really appreciate you doing this. It's really only going to take five minutes,'" Hope said. "We're going to be there an hour and a half later. He's just going to be talking to you and chatting and treating you like you're an old friend."

"How would you describe him?" the man asked.

To that, Hope had an answer that rang deep, one that is framed in his office next to a painting of the Hall of Fame slugger. "There's this poem, 'If,'" Hope said, recalling Rudyard Kipling's ode to self-discipline, which Hope's grandfather used to read to him.

If you can keep your head when all about you
Are losing theirs and blaming it on you,
If you can trust yourself when all men doubt you,
But make allowance for their doubting too;
If you can wait and not be tired by waiting,
Or being lied about, don't deal in lies,
Or being hated, don't give way to hating,
And yet don't look too good, nor talk too wise

"I always think of Hank when I read that poem," Hope said.

Upon their arrival at Aaron's home, the former Brave wanted to show the two men what he had received from the Smithsonian Institute. After his eightieth birthday, artist Ross Rossin had painted a photorealistic image of Aaron, which had been added to the National Portrait Gallery in Washington, DC. To commemorate the occasion the Smithsonian had put together a coffee table book for Aaron, and as he lifted back the cover, Hope was taken aback.

There on the first page was Kipling's "If."

"Hank, hold on," Hope said. "Did they put this poem in here?"

"That's my favorite poem," Aaron replied. "That's how I try to model my life, after that poem. So they put it in there."

A stunned Hope turned to his friend.

"Isn't this bizarre?"

It's a line from the final verse that Hope first points to when discussing Aaron: "Or walk with Kings—nor lose the common touch." He watched the future HOFer deal with the specter of Ruth's ghost hovering over him—and that was just part of the weight he carried.

"I think he gets not nearly enough credit for what he meant to the civil rights movement, being peaceful in Atlanta and far more dignified than it might have been had Hank Aaron been a different personality," Hope said. "The pressure on him was not just the Babe Ruth home run chase, but the pressure of being the African American superstar in the south, I mean any sport."

While he marched toward number 715, Aaron received vulgar hate mail and death threats and would check into hotels under a different name, sometimes staying at a different location than his teammates. He had a bodyguard, but would never give in.

"Sometimes you do things that are a little crazier than necessary, but we had that system in place," Hope said. "There was never a feeling of real threat. There was a rudeness you'd confront."

Said Bill Bartholomay, a member of the Braves ownership group, "Nobody will ever really understand—and knowing Hank he would probably downplay—the pressure on him . . . A lot of objectionable, tasteless commentary came to his attention, mostly by letter, but a lot of positives too. He just handled it in a beyond classy way, just fantastic."

Hope recalls a visit to California where he invited Aaron to visit him for drinks in a nearly empty lounge at the Sheraton-West. After Aaron had arrived, he was approached for an autograph. He obliged, but another patron took offense.

"You think you're better than the rest of us, don't you?" he said before pushing Aaron. The man was restrained and Aaron excused himself, returning to his hotel room.

"There was a lot of that little aggravation-type stuff," Hope recalls.

But Aaron maintained a dignity that in itself would become legendary.

"He never yielded to racist remarks," said former president Jimmy Carter. "He never tried to respond in any way. He never complained about it. He never made a big deal out of it. Hank was a special friend of mine."

During the home run chase, a call came from an Atlanta Little League asking if a child with leukemia could meet Aaron. The team obliged, and suddenly the Braves were inundated with calls of other dying children, and multiple families would go down before games to see him.

"You'd look and (think) 'Most of these kids aren't dying,'" Hope said. "Some of them were really sick, but most of them, people were just conning us to come down and get a reason to meet Hank Aaron."

The National League would soon adopt a rule that forbade children from being in the dugout before a game. So Hope went to Aaron and, thinking with the pressure mounting as he chased Ruth, that he could save Aaron a few minutes before a game.

"Kids aren't allowed in the dugout," Hope told him. "So all these kids that come down there because they're sick, you and I know most of them aren't sick. So we don't have to do that."

"Well, I know a lot of them aren't sick, but some of them are," Aaron replied. "I don't mind that. The time with the kids is kind of a relaxing time and it's distracting for me. I'll keep that up regardless."

Years later, Hope was approached by a man in an airport who told him that while on their way to New Orleans to get open-heart surgery for his son they stopped in Atlanta so he could meet Aaron. The boy had his picture taken with him and had a baseball signed. Less than a week later he died on an operating table and he would be buried with that baseball.

"Probably the greatest moment of his life," the man told him.

"I thought, 'That's probably the greatest statement to Hank,' because nobody knew that Hank was doing that," Hope said.

On April 8, 1974, Aaron stopped walking with kings and, as a ball went from the hands of Al Downing to those of Tom House, he became a king himself.

"This was the record of all records," Bartholomay said. "This is the record nobody thought anybody would ever catch and it was done by Hank Aaron."

In the process he would make two pitchers and a reporter—who happened to be at the right place at the right time—part of one of baseball's most celebrated moments.

*   *   *   *

"This is the young pitcher we brought up," said Elston Howard—a longtime friend of Aaron's from their Negro Leagues days—as the Yankees catcher and reigning American League MVP presented his roommate.

"I hear good things about you," Aaron said as he met Downing, a lanky left-hander who would go on that season to lead the AL in strikeouts. "You need any advice or help, you give me a call."

It was spring training 1964 and Aaron, ten years, nine All-Star appearances, and an MVP into his own career, was filling his role. Along with the likes of Ernie Banks, Willie Mays, Frank Robinson, and Billy Williams, Aaron was among the crop of black stars that followed Jackie Robinson and he was paying it forward.

"They were the guys that were responsible for the next level of young black players coming into the major leagues," Downing said, "and [they were] giving them advice on how to handle yourself up here, keeping yourself fit and ready to play, how to deal with the everyday rigors of playing in the major leagues."

Over the next decade when they saw each other they would exchange pleasantries—a "How you doing?" matched with one back—and after Downing left the Yankees for the Dodgers in 1971, their meetings took on a different focus. They faced off twenty-four times during Downing's first three seasons in Los Angeles, with Aaron collecting six hits against him with two home runs. But over that span, Downing had yet to lose a start to Atlanta, with the Dodgers going 6–0 in games he opened against the Braves in 1973. He'd been an All-Star in 1967 and a 20-game winner in 1971.

Manager Walter Alston had an easy choice when he announced, after Aaron hit number 714 two games earlier, who would start Los Angeles' first road game of the season: Downing.

The Dodgers had a future Hall of Famer in 29-year-old Don Sutton, and Andy Messersmith, who would go 20–6 that season and finish second in the Cy Young voting, but Downing was the group's elder statesman.

Plus, Downing had experience with this kind of potential circus. He was a rookie in New York when Mickey Mantle and Roger Maris chased Ruth's single-season record.

"I firstly believe that Walter Alston felt that it was a very important game, not only for us, but for everybody," Downing said. "Who was the most seasoned veteran he had on his ball club? It was me."

The pitch, Downing would later joke, was "a sinker . . . that didn't sink."

Despite the potential to be on the wrong end of history, Downing wasn't changing his approach—"I'm trying to win this ball game," he said—and there was no thought of trying to pitch around Aaron, though he did walk him in the first inning on five pitches. It drew boos from a crowd of 53,775 that included Sammy Davis Jr. and Carter, who was then Georgia's governor, and sat through a forty-five-minute pregame celebration of Aaron's career.

Though he had once been a power pitcher, at this stage in his career Downing was trying to generate groundballs. So when Aaron came up in the bottom of the fourth with Darrell Evans on first, Downing's only thoughts were on minimizing damage.

"You always think, 'Look, I'm not going out here thinking about giving up a home run. I'm going out there thinking about a double play,' because that was your stock-in-trade at the time," he said.

In those previous twenty-four meetings, Downing had struck Aaron out just once. Knowing he was going to make contact, Downing threw a sinker that he wanted to move down and away from the right-hander. Instead it elevated.

"I got a little too much of the center of the plate with that pitch," Downing said. "You're not dealing with the average hitter in baseball. You're dealing with the premier hitter in baseball and when he gets a pitch like that, his eyes had to light up 'Oh, this is it.' He's all over that pitch."

Before he strode to the plate, Aaron had a message for his young protégé, Dusty Baker. "That I can remember like it was yesterday," Baker said in 2014. "It was a cold, cold night in April. Hank told me, 'I'm going to get this over with now.' He knew every pitch that was coming. He had total recall of pitch sequences. He was as smart as they came."

"I think that was right," Aaron confirmed. "I think I made that remark and made it to Dusty maybe three or four times. I just felt within myself that eventually before the night was over I was going to hit a home run."

He did, and as the ball set sail off Aaron's 33-ounce model A99 Louisville Slugger, Baker raised his fist toward the sky and Braves radio voice Milo Hamilton made the call that resonates more than four decades later:

Henry Aaron, in the second inning walked and scored. He's sittin' on 714. Here's the pitch by Downing. Swinging.

There's a drive into left-center field. That ball is gonna be-eee . . . Outta here! It's gone! It's 715!

There's a new home run champion of all time, and it's Henry Aaron.

As Bartholomay notes, the events of that night may have all been laid out, if you look hard enough. The number 4 is said to represent those with strength, power, and stability, and it was everywhere in that moment. Aaron wore number 44, as did Downing. Atlanta was playing in their fourth game of the season in the fourth month (April) of the year on a day (8th) divisible by four and Aaron connected in the fourth inning.

"If you believe in numerology, and I never did until that night, you've got to focus on the number four," Bartholomay said.

In the Braves bullpen in that fourth inning, Tom House was instead focused on staking his ground.

They all did, each of the relievers claiming a ten-yard territory, from Jack Acker, who had the most experience in the majors and was closest to the left field foul pole (the right-handed Aaron was a notorious pull hitter) to Buzz Capra. Having pitched in 41 major-league games entering the 1974 season, Capra was the only pitcher who had logged less MLB time than House and his 71 games.

So with Capra to his left, House watched the flight of Aaron's blast.

"We all agreed beforehand that we were going to respect our territories," House said.

The ball came directly toward him. "Nothing more, nothing less," he said. "If I would have stood still, it would have hit me in the forehead." Immediately after catching it, a fishing net on an extension pole, which was being wielded by a college student sitting behind him, flew by his face.

Dodgers outfielder Bill Buckner (who would find himself inhabiting a place in baseball infamy twelve years later) had climbed the fence and was making his plea.

"Give it to me. Give it to me," Buckner screamed.

"Not really," House replied. "I'm on my way to home plate. Good luck."

The next thing House remembered he was in front of Hank, who was embracing his mother, Estella. "It's kind of fuzzy," House said. "I remember catching it and the next thing I was cognitive of was being in front of him and his mother, who was giving him a big hug, and holding it up and saying 'Here it is, Hammer.' I never really thought about keeping it at all. All I could thing about was, 'I caught it and I want to get it to him as quick as I can.'"

That it was House that had come in possession of the ball was a blessing for the Braves. Sammy Davis Jr. had offered $25,000 to whoever caught it.

"The security was prepared to identify the person that caught it and make sure they set down with them and find out what it would take to get the ball to Hank," Hope said of their plans. "But we didn't have to deal with that."

House would be rewarded. Magnavox, with whom Aaron had signed a $1 million promotional deal, gave House a home entertainment system, and the ball and Aaron's bat went to the electronics company for use in the American Freedom Train exhibit two years later. The memorabilia would be part of the ten-car rail caravan that also featured a copy of the Constitution signed by George Washington and Judy Garland's dress from *The Wizard of Oz.*

The entertainment system went with House when he moved from an Atlanta apartment to California years later, and when he eventually relocated from Coronado to Del Mar, he donated it to Goodwill. In the aftermath of 715, he also received an estimated $300 to $400 from people across the country, commending him for giving Aaron the ball.

"(They'd write) 'It's pretty cool that you gave the ball back. Here's five dollars or here's a check for . . .'" House said.

They are forever linked to Aaron, Downing and House. They are accomplices to history, a link that largely overshadows anything they've done before or since. Downing was the first black starting pitcher in Yankees history, an All-Star, and a broadcaster after he retired, but there's no escaping 715. House would go on to write or co-write nineteen instructional baseball books and pen an autobiography entitled *The Jock's Itch: The Fast-Track Private World of the Professional Ballplayer.* He also became a noted quarterback guru, working with the likes of Tom Brady and Drew Brees, and worked to transform two Indian baseball novices into pitchers in what was the basis of Disney's film *Million Dollar Arm.* But he too will always be remembered as part of Aaron's accomplishment.

"The really cool thing is that when I talk about that, being a trivia question, that's the highlight," House said. "The good news, catching Henry Aaron's 715th career [home run] was the highlight of my career. That's also the bad news, that's the highlight."

Said Downing of how often Aaron's home run comes up: "What year is this now? It's still going."

Downing and House and that April night at Atlanta Stadium were cemented from the start, but a 22-year-old reporter would see his own inclusion take on a life of its own years later.

*   *   *   *

As Aaron rounded third base after that historic blast and neared home, his teammates were waiting for him. So too was Craig Sager, a floppy-haired kid clutching a microphone and tape recorder.

A year removed from graduating from Northwestern, he was working at WSPB, an AM radio station in Sarasota, Florida. Making $95 a week as news director, he was also tasked with live updates during the morning and afternoons, and his boss made it clear: He was expected back the next morning or he would be fired.

"Oh yeah, he was serious," Sager said. "Of course then after I got back he took all the credit: 'Oh yeah, it was my idea to send him.'"

Sager would become a staple at Turner Sports as a sideline reporter for TNT and TBS, and his rise decades after Aaron's homer would make his inclusion in the oft-played highlight something of an Easter egg. "With electronic media and everything going on, YouTube, whatever, it's so easily accessible that's it's bigger now, obviously, than it ever was," Sager said.

Sager's trademark has long been his outlandish clothing, a palette of velvet, plaid, stripes, and fluorescent colors. NBA All-Star Kevin Garnett took special exception to one pink suit, telling Sager, "You take this outfit home and you burn it."

Making a fashion statement wasn't on his mind as he wore his old dad's trench coat, a choice made for combating the cold and rain. But it also made him impossible to miss. As Aaron rounded third and stepped onto home plate Sager worked his way past Los Angeles catcher Joe Ferguson into the scrum of Braves and followed Aaron and those offering their congratulations while he made his way to his parents.

Back in college Sager had dressed as Willie the Wildcat, with his role as a mascot making him used to being on the field—"I used to run around on the field all the time," he said—so he thought nothing of running into that celebration.

"I don't know, out of instinct, I just went out there," Sager said. "When you look at the video, sure it looks like 'What the hell is he doing out there?' But at the time, I had the microphone and I just felt like I wanted to get in there and see what was going on and record whatever I could."

He captured House delivering the ball and the joy in the voice of Aaron's mother, who was escorted by Bartholomay. The owner was with Estella and Herbert Aaron and immediately after the homer, "helped get her over our little guard in front of where we were sitting." Mother and son embraced—and Sager, and Sager alone, had it all on tape.

"I knew I had something special in there, because of just the sound with his mother, you know, everybody else, Tom House saying 'Here's the ball. Here's the ball.' The recording of the moment and all that was great, but I had sound that nobody else had and nobody else would have had," Sager said.

Months later, before the All-Star Game in Pittsburgh, Sager approached Aaron at a table with the intent of giving him a tape of the call. Thinking he wanted an autograph, Aaron showed little interest.

"That's okay," Aaron told him. "I've seen it all."

But when Sager finally played the tape for him, Aaron remembered the kid with the trench coat and tape recorder.

"That was kind of a bond right away, because he realized I hadn't given it to someone, I hadn't sold out on him, and I was just giving it to him," Sager said.

The two stayed close over the years, phoning on the anniversary of the home run, and in 1996 Aaron and Sager made a trip to Cuba. After MLB stopped Braves owner Ted Turner from taking the Braves to play against the island's national team, which won gold in baseball at that year's Summer Olympics in Atlanta, Turner opted instead to have the next best thing.

"They won't let me take the Braves over there," Turner told Cuban president Fidel Castro. "I'm going to send Hank over to do some clinics for you guys."

Upon telling Aaron, Turner suggested that he reach out to Sager, who worked for Turner-owned CNN and TBS for the 1991 Pan American Games in Havana.

"Talk to him, go with him, he'll take you," Turner told Aaron.

Sager went and discussed the trip with Aaron, telling him "Oh, the people are great. We'll have a great time."

Unable to tell anyone they were going due to travel and trade restrictions, Aaron and Sager flew to the Bahamas before making their way to Cuba, where they went to a number of small towns to put on youth baseball clinics. Sager would give a brief introduction of why they were there before turning things over to Aaron. They moved from destination to destination, with word spreading before their arrival.

"The next town would know we were coming. It was like something you could just do in a movie," Sager said.

"There was no way you would think that was live in the way of spontaneity that you could have something happen like that."

Still, pulling up in an expensive car, in a place where such things are rarely seen, created some confusion about who was inside.

"People would say 'Oh, somebody big? Is it Fidel?'" Sager recalls. "Then they'd hear it was baseball and they'd say 'Willie Mays! Willie Mays!' and Hank would get out of the car and (they'd say) 'Willie Mays!' and he'd say 'No, I'm Hank Aaron' (and they'd say) 'Oh, Hank Aaron!'"

Beyond baseball, Sager also helped Aaron navigate the street shops of the Malecón. He had instructed Aaron to bring jeans that he could exchange for boxes of cigars.

"You're going into these houses with no security, nobody around him," Sager said. "Going in there and not being able to understand the language but being able to get Hank cigars. We just had a great time."

* * * *

Fireworks filled the sky, and an electronic sign in the stadium flashed "Move Over Babe Here Comes Henry." But there was neither pomp nor circumstance in Aaron's first public comments as he stepped to the microphone. "I just thank God it's all over," he said.

He was presented with a new Cadillac from the Atlanta Chamber of Commerce, while Governor Carter gave Aaron a license plate that said HR715. It wasn't the gift of a new car that would gain the most notoriety.

"I gave him a ten-dollar license plate and then in *Encyclopedia Americana* they had a picture of me giving him a license plate and didn't mention the fact that he got an eight-thousand-dollar Cadillac from the Chamber of Commerce," Carter recalls, laughing.

While Aaron's thoughts were centered on relief, Hope's were too, to a degree.

The streaking fad of the 1970s was one of the Braves' biggest concerns in the run-up to Aaron's record-breaking homer. They had one streaker, a woman who removed a raincoat in the upper deck of the stadium. Asked how he'd like to handle it, Hope replied "Well, tell her put her clothes on. Nobody noticed her, they were all watching Hank run around the bases."

The real fear came when 17-year-olds Cliff Courtenay and Britt Gaston jumped onto the field along the first-base line and caught up with Aaron as he rounded second. They patted him on the back before running back down the first-base line. They were both arrested, though charges were dropped.

"It could have been a lot worse," Aaron said in 2010. "They were having fun with it as kids."

Said Hope, "I think what happened in hindsight is that everybody got so caught up in watching the home run that they weren't doing their job. That was a scary thought when they ran out on the field."

More than anything, though, the end of Aaron hunting down Ruth came with tangible realities for Hope and the Braves.

"When it was over there was a little bit, 'Is that all there is?'" Hope said. "You had this big buildup and what's the old line Ray Kroc says, 'It's more fun when you're chasing it than when you finally get it.' I think there was a little bit of that."

He wasn't being selfish. It meant no more sellouts and no more hype. He and his staff had put together a pamphlet detailing Aaron's career, and had issued hundreds of press credentials per day.

They had set up a system where they'd line up fifteen-minute interviews with major media and then have pre- and postgame press conferences for home games. During the last season before 715, the Braves traveled to Los Angeles, and unbeknownst to them, a group of writers from Tokyo showed up wanting to interview Aaron.

"We thought 'Well, we've got to do something,'" Hope said.

They shortened other interviews to give the Japanese media extra time, but with the need for translators, it slowed down the process. Aaron eventually went to Hope and told him "Bob, I've talked to them and I told them you've heard every answer to every question I've ever been asked, and they're going to interview you as if you're me because they have more questions and I have to do these other interviews."

Hope sat in the visiting dugout for close to an hour answering questions.

"After about five minutes, I thought I was Hank Aaron," he said, laughing.

*   *   *   *

On April 8, 2014, the fortieth anniversary of Aaron's record-setting night, Commissioner Bud Selig stood at a podium in Turner Field, *715* mowed into the outfield while fans in Aaron jerseys held baseball-shaped signs with the numerals 1 through 715.

In an address before Aaron would speak, Selig called him "ideally suited to become Babe Ruth's heir" and said that "because he is the living embodiment of the American spirit . . . Baseball is forever our national pastime because of people like Henry Aaron."

Given the cloud of performance-enhancing drugs that hang over Barry Bonds, who would pass Aaron's career record of 755 on August 7, 2007, this was as close to taking sides as it gets from an active commissioner.

"I'm always in a sensitive spot there, but I've said that myself and I'll just leave it at that," Selig told reporters afterward.

Two months earlier Aaron had broken his hip after slipping on ice outside his home, and required surgery. But with former teammates Baker, House, Ralph Garr, Phil Niekro, Marty Perez, and Ron Reed on hand, along with retired Braves broadcaster Pete Van Wieren (who died four months later after a battle with cancer) and Cliff Courtenay (Britt Gaston died in 2011 at age fifty-five), the 80-year-old Aaron made the trip, using a walker as he made his way to the microphone.

"Forty years ago, if I would have known this was going to happen this way, I would have hit the home run earlier, probably," he quipped. "I just want to say on behalf of Hank Aaron, my wife, and of course, all of my fans, I just want to say thank you so very much for all your kindness for these many years."

Jerseys were unveiled from Atlanta-area college and pro teams, with Falcons owner Arthur Blank, former Georgia coach Vince Dooley, and ex–Georgia Tech coach Bill Curry among those presenting Aaron with their respective teams with number 44 and Aaron's name.

"The game of baseball was a way that I relaxed myself each year that I went on the field for twenty-three

Hank Aaron's 755 career home runs would stand as the major-league record for thirty-three years. (*Lauren Gerson/LBJ Foundation*)

years," Aaron said. "I gave baseball everything that I had. Everything, every ounce of my ability to play the game, I tried to play to make you the fans appreciate me more. Thank you."

A Downing pitch led to the occasion, and it was one that punctuated this ceremony, with the left-hander throwing out the ceremonial first pitch. Outside Turner Field, in the parking lot where Atlanta–Fulton County Stadium once stood, is a monument marking the landing spot of number 715, surrounded by part of the park's outfield wall.

But Aaron's career was more than just homers. Even without those 755 long balls, he would still have 3,016 hits, including 2,294 singles, and was a .305 career hitter. He also won Gold Gloves from 1958 to 1960. But he says he takes the most pride in his RBI record of 2,297 and never striking out more than 100 times in a season.

"There was absolutely no time that anybody could say, 'Well he hit a lot of home runs but he struck out a lot of times,'" Aaron said in 2014. "That was not to be. That was one of the most embarrassing moments of my life, to go to the plate and strike out once or twice and not be able to make contact."

Aaron didn't say much to his teammates the night of 715. There was a dugout phone call from President Richard Nixon before his postgame press conference, and later Aaron was toasted in private by teammates with Moët & Chandon champagne.

At the press conference, Aaron took to the table in the middle of the clubhouse, drawing laughs as he looked toward the locker next to his. He said, "I promised Ralph Garr I was going to do it, because so many newspaper men had been hanging around my locker, I was afraid he'd get trampled to death."

He would go on to thank them for their patience, and again say he was glad it was over. A man of few words,

Aaron lived up to that billing, even after taking down one of sports' most hallowed records.

"We played baseball every day and being around Henry (and) what he did every day, he had this great knack for making it seem simple," House said. "You never realized how much he contributed to a game until you read the box score that night or the next morning. He was just quietly confident and it was the same thing breaking the record."

Chapter Two

Ted Turner Shakes Up the Game

The Christian Council of Metropolitan Atlanta wanted to talk.

In less than two seasons since Ted Turner had purchased the team in 1976, the Braves held Ostrich Race Night—twice—had Home Run King Hank Aaron wheel a mechanized bathtub against other celebrities, and staged a mattress-stacking contest. No one raised any concerns over those events, but when word got out that the team would be putting on a wet T-shirt contest, it was a different matter.

"This is our out," public relations director Bob Hope, who was in charge of the team's promotions, told Turner as they went to meet with the city's church leaders. "This is it. I told you we're not going to be able to have this thing."

The idea—which seems deplorable and woefully politically incorrect in modern times—came from a group of students the Braves used to plan their college nights. The World Mattress-Stacking Championship had been a success; an estimated one hundred mattresses were on-site as the team reached out to fraternities and sororities to take part. Looking for a similar buzz for their next promotion, the students threw out half-baked ideas.

"We'll have a best butt contest," one male said.

"You can't do that," Hope replied.

"Well, let's judge the breasts," another recommended.

"You can't do that, guys," Hope said. "There's no way."

"Well, why don't you let them wear T-shirts," a student shot back.

"You can't do that," Hope answered.

"Well," came the final suggestion, "we can wet down the T-shirts."

The students began laughing and Hope, realizing the meeting was going nowhere, said, "Guys, we just don't have an idea."

Back in his office, Hope had received a call from *Atlanta Constitution* columnist Lewis Grizzard, who was looking to write about whatever promotion the Braves were cooking up.

"Lewis, we don't have one right now," Hope said. "We just had a meeting and I can tell you one we aren't going to do."

"You can't make those decisions," Grizzard told him upon hearing about the wet T-shirt contest. "Let the readers make the decision."

Grizzard wrote a column asking readers to weigh in and the response, he would tell Hope, was that Atlanta wanted to see it. "It was just some overwhelming thing," Hope recalls.

They decided to promote the contest—which would include $500 for the winner—for the May 20 game against the Cubs, and ticket sales began to take off. But the Braves were certain they wouldn't actually go through with it.

"They're going to stop us as we get closer to it," Hope told Turner. "There's no way. People are going to object."

That's when the Metro Atlanta Christian Council came calling, days before the event was scheduled.

"They're going to meet with us and we're going be gracious and we're going to say we're just trying so hard to draw crowds and we just lost seventeen games in a row," Hope told his boss as he and Turner drove to the meeting. "We just are trying so hard and we just made a mistake. We're sorry and we're not going to have it."

The council certainly did have its concerns. They wanted it moved to after the game so that families with children could leave . . . and they wanted to designate their own judge.

"We're going to have to have this thing," a stunned Turner said as they left.

That night's game was delayed two and a half hours by rain, but during the sixth inning an announcement came that registration was open for the wet T-shirt contest. Forty-three contestants signed up and were hosed down, after the game finished well past midnight, with thirty judges—including the Metro Atlanta Christian Council's representative—on hand.

The winner was the 24-year-old daughter of a Methodist minister.

Expecting backlash, Hope sensed it was coming when he received a phone call from Phillies promotions director Frank Sullivan, who said team owner Ruly Carpenter wanted a set of pictures from the contest.

"I thought 'Oh, man. I'm getting kicked out of baseball,'" Hope said.

Days later Carpenter himself called. He wanted three hundred more sets of photos to send to his friends.

"We did some things that were shameful, no question," Hope said.

In 1978, Dale Murphy would arrive and blossom into a star, and the team turned into a national brand thanks to TBS. Those early days of Turner's run also included Phil Niekro having some of the most productive seasons of his Hall of Fame career, a National League West crown in 1982, a nineteen-inning epic with the Mets on July 4, 1985, and Bob Horner hitting four home runs on July 6, 1986. But more often than not, in that period, the Braves needed all the help they could get.

"He was doing everything he could to get people to come to the games," said former president Jimmy Carter, a close friend of Turner's. "I think one of the games he only had 1,500 people show up. When I was playing softball against my brother, Billy—we were both pitchers in slow-pitch softball—we had more people watching us than went to the Braves that game."

In Turner's first season, 1976, they averaged 10,107 fans per game (twentieth out of twenty-four teams) and finished 32 games back in the National League West; the following year they drew 10,771 (twenty-second) and finished 37 games back. Over the first fifteen years of the Turner era they were a sub-.500 team twelve times and lost 92 or more in nine seasons.

"It was certainly zany, there was more of an entertainment component to it," Hope said. "We didn't have money, so a lot of the stuff we did—ostriches were cheap, fireworks we did enough of them that they were fairly cheap—we had the things we knew would draw attention to individual games."

Eventually, Turner would adopt a largely hands-off approach to baseball, appointing Stan Kasten team president, and he in turn would bring in proven commodities like Bobby Cox and John Schuerholz (Kasten's involvement would end after the team was swallowed up by Time Warner in 1996 and ultimately sold to Liberty Media in 2007). But the early version of Ted Turner, Owner—before he was married to Jane Fonda, and named *Time* magazine's Man of the Year—was one of the franchise's biggest attractions. Before the home opener in 1977, a parade of Atlanta personalities took part in a ceremony, but only three earned standing ovations: Aaron, recently-retired Falcons linebacker Tommy Nobis, and Turner.

"His deal was, which was pretty smart, that if you're famous, the world comes to you," Hope said. "People come to you with ideas they want to do and you can see all of them. If you're not famous, then you've got to figure out who you want to go see. That being a magnet because he was famous meant a lot to him back then."

Hence Turner rolling a baseball across first base to home plate with his nose in a competition with the Phillies' Tug McGraw (and winning), racing an ostrich, and losing to a local columnist (an upset Turner said, "One lap. How the hell can you determine the fastest ostrich in one lap?"), and positioning himself as a participatory Bill Veeck.

"One time last year, I just decided to run out with the ball girl when she went to sweep the bases after the fifth inning," Turner told *Playboy* in an August 1978 interview. "I swept the bases, then did a flip at third base. You want to know why I bought the Braves? Because the stadium is one big playpen where I can have 53,000 of my friends over for a little fun."

He would also try to get Andy Messersmith to have his jersey read CHANNEL 17 to promote his Superstation WTBS (Channel 17 in Atlanta) before MLB stepped in and stopped him; and he installed a $2 million instant replay screen that irked a crew of umpires who threatened to walk off the field in two straight games. They took exception to having pitches replayed and then objected to a replay of a close call at home plate.

But none of the antics by the man dubbed the Mouth of the South and Captain Outrageous—among his other nicknames—have had as much of a lasting impact as his one-game stint as manager on May 11, 1977, at Pittsburgh's Three Rivers Stadium.

After losing a doubleheader to the Pirates that ran the Braves' losing streak to sixteen and dropped them to 8–21, Turner gave manager Dave Bristol ten days off to relax at his Andrews, North Carolina, home so the owner could take over and figure out what was ailing the team.

Turner, then 38, took the field wearing number 27 when he encountered Niekro.

"I was pitching that day, and I remember Ted came out of the clubhouse with the Braves uniform on, and I just got through hitting in the batting cage pregame in Pittsburgh, and I came behind the cage to wait for my next turn and Ted came out and I was standing right next to him," Niekro said. "I just joked to him, I said 'Hey, Ted, what spot you got me hitting in today?' He said 'Hell, I don't care. You want to lead off? You want to hit third or fourth?' I said 'We just lost sixteen in a row. I think you'd better keep me in the ninth spot. (That) may upset some players.'"

Atlanta's skid would reach seventeen, and Turner's stint as manager came to an end as the next day National League president Chub Feeney cited Major League Rule 20E, which prohibits either manager or players of a club from holding stock or ownership in their teams. Asked by the Braves to review the decision, baseball commissioner Bowie Kuhn backed Feeney.

"Given Mr. Turner's lack of familiarity with game operations, I do not think it is in the best interest of baseball to serve in his requested capacity," Kuhn told reporters.

In a brief phone conversation Kuhn would tell Turner he'd have to convince him he should be allowed in the dugout. Turner, though, thought the Braves' place in the standings should be enough.

"If we were in a pennant race or something I could understand being turned down," he said at the time. "But we're already fifteen and a half games out of first place, three and a half games in last place."

Turner had already gotten under Kuhn's skin. Kuhn had suspended him in January 1977 for a year for tampering. At a New York cocktail party in 1976, Turner had challenged Giants co-owner Bob Lurie to outbid him when San Francisco outfielder-to-be Gary Matthews became available. Turner landed Matthews for $1.75 million over five years—and a $10,000 fine from MLB, along with the loss in that year's free-agent draft.

"I'm thankful he didn't order me shot," said Turner. "I don't really think we did anything seriously wrong [in the process of drafting and signing Matthews.]"

He appealed and the ban was temporarily lifted in March—it was during that window that Turner managed the team—pending a hearing in US District Court. But Turner did little to aid his cause, telling one of Kuhn's lawyers, Nick Wertheimer, during cross-examination in the first day of testimony, "After this is over, you keep that up, and you'll get a knuckle sandwich."

Unsurprisingly, federal judge Newell Edenfield upheld the ban, writing, "The commissioner has general authority, without rules or directives, to punish both clubs and/or personnel for any act or conduct which, in his judgment, is 'not in the best interests of baseball'—a power given to the commissioner by Major League Agreement.

"He (Kuhn) has made his finding that Turner's conduct was out of character. The court knows of no authority which prevented him from making it, and cannot say his decision was either arbitrary or wrong."

Turner's ban, which would have run until March 23, 1978, was ultimately lifted three months early at the December Winter Meetings in Honolulu. But in that time away Turner stayed in the limelight, captaining the *Courageous*—a 12-metre class yacht—to a four-race sweep in the America's Cup series in Australia and beating out Ted Hood, who had won the event with the *Courageous* three years earlier.

Fitting a man who once said "If I only had a little humility, I would be perfect," his stance on what he accomplished at sea was, well, without a shred of humility.

"I was an innocent man serving time," he told *Playboy*. "I mean, Jesus Christ would have been considered just another long-haired hippie freak if he hadn't been crucified. The folks weren't impressed with healing the sick, feeding the multitudes bread and fish or anything else, except maybe the walking on water. But when he got crucified, that gave him his big start. Especially when he came up again three days later—that was a real good show. The America's Cup wouldn't have been famous if I hadn't been suspended."

The ban only increased his rebel image, but Hope alleges that it wasn't the Turner vs. Kuhn battle it looked to be.

"He needed a good excuse to not be [in baseball], so he sort of orchestrated him getting banned from baseball," Hope said.

The Braves had a campaign with Burger King in which they had patrons from metro Atlanta and throughout the South fill out protest forms that would be sent to the commissioner calling for Turner to be reinstated. Hope said Kuhn allowed the Braves to hire his secretary and some of the assistants in his office and they compiled lists of everyone who sent those letters so the team could in turn send them ticket information.

"So if there was collusion, there was collusion going at all different levels," Hope said. "Baseball was kind of smaller and we all sort of understood each other and got along and hardly anybody was completely offended by Ted, it was just his approach to promoting the game."

Ted, as everyone referred to him, was different. He would shower in the locker room after the games and ride home on the bus with the players after games. In Turner's first home game as owner, Ken Henderson hit a home run against the Reds, and Turner jumped out of his seat and ran onto the field to shake Henderson's hand.

"There's only one owner in baseball who's like Ted Turner—and that's Ted Turner," Braves third baseman Jerry Royster told the *Miami News* in April 1977. "With all the money he has, you'd expect him to be a white-shirt-and-tie guy. But he's just like you and I. He doesn't go for that fancy-Dan stuff, sitting up in his office watching the baseball games while smoking a cigar. Ted'll smoke his cigar but he'll have his T-shirt off, a beer in his hand, and a Braves hat on his head. That's Ted."

Recalled Niekro, "He was the only owner that would come in the clubhouse after a game every night and whether we won or lost, kick his shoes off, and we would talk about baseball. He'd come in with shorts and tennis shoes with no socks and a T-shirt and set down and be one of the players."

He was a man of the people, and Turner knew exactly what they wanted. Late in the 1977 season, when the Braves were on their way to losing an Atlanta-record 101 games, a sparse crowd was on hand vs. the Padres. "There were more ushers in the stadium than people (in the stands)," said outfielder/third baseman Barry Bonnell, a rookie on that team.

Turner got on the intercom and instructed fans to move down into the box seats behind home plate and "Anybody that comes down gets a free bottle of champagne."

"Everybody came down and they just had a party behind home plate," Bonnell said. "I'm telling you, it was better for us. We had some fans there, but you wouldn't have been able to tell. There were probably a couple hundred fans scattered all over the place. So then we brought them back behind the plate and then they started getting noisy, it was like we had a crowd, suddenly."

Said Murphy, "I think probably everyone who knows Ted would probably say they'd never known anyone like him and especially me, not in his world until I got with the Braves. Even in the minor leagues we were aware of Ted, but it wasn't until I got to Atlanta where our worlds came together. He was a man of flamboyance and outspokenness that I couldn't imagine."

Technically, Eddie Robinson, John Alevizos, Bill Lucas, and John Mullen were the Braves general managers until Bobby Cox took over in 1986, but Murphy remembers in those early days dealing directly with Turner when it came to his contract negotiations.

"I don't think that's typically the way an organization chart works," Murphy said. "You negotiate, as I understand it, with the GM. Sometimes you've got, the GM has to get approval, but then, you know, we were bypassing the GM at times. I do remember a few times my agent would say, 'Well, let's go talk to Ted. That's how it's done here.'"

On the topic of GMs, Lucas would be at the center of one of Turner's strangest fights. The first black general manager when Turner appointed him in 1976, Lucas died of a brain hemorrhage and cardiac arrest after an aneurysm ruptured in his neck. At the time, Lucas was involved in bitter talks to keep third baseman Horner in Atlanta and Turner allegedly blamed Horner's agent, Bucky Woy, for his death. The agent in turn filed a $17 million defamation suit against the owner.

"He as much as pulled the trigger of the gun, almost," Turner told a US District Court jury. "I really do not believe Bucky Woy intended to kill Bill Lucas . . . he probably didn't know he was causing (Lucas' death) . . . I didn't ever say he was guilty of murder."

After deliberating for an hour, the jury ruled in favor of Turner.

"I told the truth and when you tell the truth it's not slander," Turner said after the verdict.

Barry Bonnell, an outfielder/third baseman who spent the first three years of his major-league career (1977–1979) with the Braves, was close with Turner. Both were Cincinnati natives, and Bonnell's parents would often pick up Turner's mother, Florence, and the three would go to games together, sitting next to Ted. Bonnell and Turner hunted together, with the player flying his plane down to the owner's south Georgia plantation, and Turner gave him a loan to buy a house.

"I had a real good relationship with Ted," Bonnell said. "He treated me like I was one of his own kids."

That included the offseason, when Bonnell worked with Turner's small UHF television station WTGC, where the two would often have lunch together in Turner's office.

On one of these occasions Bonnell walked in and Turner was on the phone. Turner put his finger to his lips and directed Bonnell to sit down and he listened as the Braves owner discussed satellite transponders with an executive from Time Warner. It was that technology that allowed Turner to originate the "superstation," as he transmitted to cable systems nationwide. (The station would change its name on August 27, 1979, when it acquired the call letters WTBS from the Massachusetts Institute of Technology's student radio station for $50,000 in donations—$25,000 when it picked a new call sign and $25,000 more when the Federal Communications Commission granted Turner's request.)

"I sat down and listened to the entire conversation about the future of cable TV," Bonnell said.

When he was traded to the Blue Jays on December 5, 1979, along with Joey McLaughlin and Pat Rockett for Chris Chambliss and Luis Gomez, Bonnell saw what Turner truly had up his sleeve.

The owner called Bonnell and told him, "I tried to keep you around. I think it's a bad move, but I don't run the team. I want you to come over and have lunch with me." After they ate, Turner had something to show him, and they climbed into Turner's car and drove to a construction site, which at that point was little more than a hole in the ground with bulldozers pushing dirt around.

"This is going to make or break me right here," Turner said.

"What is it?" asked Bonnell.

"Well, it's twenty-four-hour news."

"Ted, I'm sorry man," Bonnell told him, "but there's no way that's going to work."

Turner had his doubters in those days, though he may have brought some of that himself.

It was in the Winter Meetings after the '75 season when Hope first found out that Turner was purchasing the Braves from Bill Bartholomay for $10 million. Bartholomay and the Chicago-based LaSalle Corporation were close to selling to a group led by former Red Sox executive Alevizos (who would later become Atlanta's GM), who were intent on uprooting the franchise to Toronto. Instead, Bartholomay, who had just brought the Braves to the Southeast from Milwaukee in 1966, pushed to keep the team in place and they instead sold to Turner for less than Alevizos's group was offering.

Walking up a staircase in a hotel in Hollywood, Florida, Hope was approached by a colleague who said "Bob, Bob, Ted Turner's buying the Braves."

"Oh, my God," Hope recalls saying. "This is crazy. I can't work for him."

Despite the relative weak signal of WTCG, Turner acquired the rights to broadcasting the Braves in 1973, giving ownership $600,000 for the rights to sixty games a season beginning in 1974. He began going on sales calls, and Hope would often go with him as a team representative, getting a firsthand look at Turner's tactics, which included standing on a chair singing "Heart" from *Damn Yankees*.

"We really don't need sales presentations," Turner told him. "Just talk them into buying TV time."

After purchasing the team, Turner spoke at a banquet and, as Hope recalls, "gave his most bizarre of all bizarre speeches he had ever given." Turner stood looking at the candelabras on each side of the head table, the candles on one side noticeably shorter than the other and Turner couldn't take his eyes off them.

"Why would that happen?" he said, pointing.

When Turner was done, an Atlanta businessman approached Hope and told him "Bob, your new boss could be crazy."

"I've sort of thought about that," Hope replied.

"And he might fire you," the man told him.

Hope's mind had already gone there. One month into the season, he had fired Robinson and replaced him with Alevizos—a move that would last four months before Turner went with Lucas—and Turner also let go of the team's head of ticket sales along with others.

"I've thought about that too," Hope said. "In fact, we're having lunch tomorrow and I'm worried that might be what he's going to do."

"Well let me tell you something. There's no shame in getting fired," the man told him. "The only shame is if you strikeout with the bat on your shoulder. While you've got your job, you give him everything he can handle."

The next day, Turner walked into the stadium club and when he walked over to Hope, the public relations director jumped out of his seat and poked his finger into Turner's chest.

"Ted, let me tell you something," Hope said, disclosing that it took every bit of nerve he had. "Before we get started, I'm really worried about you," Hope said.

"What do you mean?" Turner asked.

"I'm a very aggressive promoter and I just don't know if you can keep up," Hope proclaimed.

Together they helped to define the Braves in their post–Hank Aaron form. Wedlock and Headlock Night— which combined a mass wedding on the field that included thirty-four couples, followed by a wrestling match—Karl Wallenda walking across the stadium on a tightrope, frog jumping, and a local disc jockey diving headfirst into the world's largest ice cream sundae (and nearly drowning), were all the by-product of their partnership.

"We'd do all these crazy promotions and we just did this stupid, stupid, stupid stuff and we just thought they were brilliant and Ted thought they were brilliant," Hope said.

Hindsight and the cushion of years have changed their stance on that brilliance, with many of those promotions an impossibility in this age, especially that wet T-shirt contest. In a conversation a few years ago, Hope and Turner were discussing that very fact.

"Ted, think of all those crazy things we did and we always thought they were so brilliant," Hope said. "You look back and really, they were kind of stupid."

"Bob," Turner replied, "when people are still talking about what you did thirty years later and didn't hurt anybody, it was a good idea."

When Turner bought the Braves he made a bold promise during his press conference. "Getting into the World Series in five years is my objective," he said. "But it takes time to build a winning baseball team. Time, money, and effort."

Instead they would go through two managers, lose 460 games, and finish sixth in the division four times. But Turner—with Hope at his side—would set the standard in an era engulfed by marketing brainstorms.

As Turner wrote in his autobiography *Call Me Ted* of his ill-fated attempt to have Messersmith be a walking commercial for his TV station, "It was fun while it lasted and we drummed up publicity in the meantime."

Chapter Three

Dale Murphy: The Bridge

She had lost both of her arms and her left leg had been severed below the knee, the result of tripping over a 20,000-volt power line that fell during a rare spring snowstorm in March 1983, one that had dumped nearly eight inches of snow on Atlanta.

Doctors at Scottish Rite Children's Hospital would operate on 6-year-old Elizabeth Smith for six hours, discovering infectious tissue in her limbs, which caused them to further amputate her leg and remove her arms to the shoulder joint.

During her recovery she received a visitor: Dale Murphy. The Braves outfielder was with his son, who was undergoing surgery.

Months later they would meet again as Smith sat in the Fulton County Stadium stands on a June afternoon before a game against the Giants and Murphy gave her a T-shirt and hat. As he talked to Smith, the nurse suggested Murphy give her something else.

"Why don't you hit a home run for Elizabeth?" she said.

Murphy replied, "If I hit one, it will be for you."

He did. Then he did it again.

Murphy, who had gone deep just four times in his previous 115 plate appearances, hit a two-run homer off Andy McGaffigan in the third inning, then added a solo shot in the sixth. He supplied all of Atlanta's offense in a 3–2 win.

It was his Babe Ruth moment, in line with the promise the slugger made in 1926 to 11-year-old Johnny Sylvester, who suffered from inflammation near his brain after being tossed from a horse. On a ball delivered to the boy, the Yankees legend scrawled "I'll knock a homer for you in Wednesday's game." He would go on to hit three.

Murphy wasn't channeling the Bambino, but word had already spread through the media about his promise. The two-time National League MVP says it wasn't bravado; he was simply reacting after being taken off guard by the nurse's request.

"It was pretty quick thinking on my part," Murphy recalls, laughing. "'If I hit one, it will be for you'. . . I don't like to exaggerate things, but the gist of the story is real."

Humbleness. Self-effacement. The legend of Dale Murphy was built on these pillars as much as it is his prolific numbers.

"Just a person that everybody aspires to be," said former teammate Barry Bonnell. "He's honest and forthright and everything you hear about him is absolutely true."

For a generation Murphy was the Braves, their marquee player as they became a national product thanks to TBS's reach and the bridge between the eras of Hank Aaron and the team of the '90s.

"We had a real unique thing," Murphy said. "We were on cable TV everywhere. It was a real remarkable thing back during that time."

Atlanta finished below .500 in 11 of Murphy's 15 seasons, including losing 101 games in 1977 and 106 in 1988. Just once did he make the postseason as a Brave as they were swept out of the National League Championship Series by the Cardinals.

But Murphy rose above that largely down period for the franchise, making seven All-Star Games, winning five Gold Gloves and MVPs in 1982 and '83. He would hit 264 of his 398 career homers in an eight-year span.

"(My dad) would tell me Murph stories about how he played so hard, so well, on a team that would just lose 100 games a year and what that meant to him, to show up every day and play, knowing you're going to get beat, destroyed, whatever," said veteran outfielder Jeff Francoeur, an Atlanta area native, who wore number 3 with the Phillies in 2015 in Murphy's honor. "He would still show up every day, ready to go."

Murphy played the game of baseball like he's lived every aspect of his life, with personal conviction.

Mr. Nice Guy. Mr. Too Good To Be True. It's that persona that has defined Murphy. But what drove it home was that it was not an act, much to the chagrin of a reporter who in 1979 asked if Murphy acted in private like he pretended to act while in the public eye. Murphy worked with the Cystic Fibrosis Foundation and Huntington's Disease Society of America and spent off days with children in the hospital. In 2005 he wrote *The Scouting Report*, a guide to negotiating life as a professional athlete.

"The phrase 'Wrong place at the right time,' when an athlete says that, I kind of just chuckle," Murphy said. "It's a personal decision. You just, 'I'm not going to go there tonight or do that.' People will take advantage of you as a professional athlete and it's a matter of making decisions really, one decision after another, and that's true in life, really. Not just the locker room."

He said it—and he lived it.

Murphy would refuse to give television interviews in the locker room unless fully dressed. Not a smoker or a drinker, he would pay teammates' checks at dinner as long as alcohol wasn't on the tab, and he didn't abide cursing. He once famously told a fan heckling the umpires, "Say whatever you want, but stop the swearing!"

Murphy's clean-cut way of life made all the more natural a change that began while he was traveling through the South Carolina countryside in 1975.

$$* \quad * \quad * \quad *$$

As the Greenwood Braves climbed aboard the old school bus after games against Class-A Western Carolina League teams, Bonnell would settle in for another long road trip. With no overhead lights in the bus he would turn on his flashlight, tape it to the seat in front of him, and read *The Book of Mormon* as they traveled through towns like Anderson, Rock Hill, Salisbury, and Thomasville.

"It attracted attention when you read something in the middle of the night with a light, so some people would come around asking about it," said Bonnell, who played for the Braves from 1977 to 1979.

They'd talk, and if they'd ask, Bonnell would tell them about the book and what it meant to be a Mormon.

All the while, Murphy would listen, time and again sitting near enough to Bonnell to hear, but never engaging in the discussion.

Typically one of the first ones on the bus, Bonnell decided one day to wait until Murphy had taken his seat. He followed him on, sat down next to Murphy, and followed his same routine: flashlight and scripture.

"He started asking questions about it," Bonnell said. "It wasn't too long after the missionaries were talking to him and I baptized him the day after the season was over that year."

Murphy was torn. Like most young, unmarried Mormons the 19-year-old wanted to go on a two-year mission, but he also had a contract with the Braves, one that while he mulled over his future, remained unsigned.

Dale's father, Charles, received a phone call from Braves owner Ted Turner, who bluntly asked him what was wrong with his son. Was it girl problems?

"No, he's got a religious problem," Charles Murphy told the *Ensign*, the magazine of the LDS church. "He has wanted to go on a mission for his church. And he also wants to play ball. He'll do the right thing. But don't push him; his religion means a great deal to him."

Turner responded, "I'm going to call him and I'm going to tell him, if he'll sign this contract—and he knows it is a good one—I'll give him a chance to convert me, my wife and children, and my aunt to the Mormon church. . . . Then I'm going to tell him if he doesn't sign, all these people, plus my mother, are going to commit suicide."

Recalls Murphy, "Oh, I got a phone call from Ted. Yeah, he wasn't very excited about the idea."

Murphy's talks with local Church of Latter-Day Saints leaders ultimately helped him realize the good he could do for the Mormon faith through his work on the baseball field.

"I went through some soul searching and talked to a lot of people and did a lot of praying about it and just decided [to stay in baseball]," Murphy said.

Invested in the church, he was looking for the same thing in a wife. During the 1978 offseason, Murphy enrolled for a semester at Brigham Young University in Provo, Utah, where he met a cheerleader named Nancy Thomas. The only problem was she was dating Murphy's roommate, basketball player Steve Craig.

After the two broke up, Murphy and Thomas began dating—Craig, meanwhile, would marry Mormon royalty in Marie Osmond—and the two began a long-distance relationship conducted over the phone or while she was visiting Bonnell and his wife in Atlanta. They would be married October 29, 1970, in the Salt Lake Temple and have eight children—seven boys and a girl.

In the major leagues, Murphy's lifestyle stood out. He didn't go out to bars with teammates, and other players were known to refrain from colorful language around him. But he never felt that his religion was an issue.

"I look back at my career and received nothing but respect from my teammates," he said. "You get together as a team and there are twenty-five different feelings about everything: religious backgrounds, economic backgrounds, upbringings, things like that. I found that as I respected others, respect was generally paid back in my direction."

Bonnell, though, remembers one situation while they were in the minors when he and Murphy encountered a misunderstanding that centered around their chosen faith.

After a game in Montreal against an All-Star team they were fed hot dogs; later that night in their hotel, Bonnell came down with food poisoning. Murphy called former trainer Dave Pursley to help get his teammate to the hospital—though the weak-stomached Murphy would need some assistance of his own, as he passed out and hit his chin, requiring stitches.

"I thought I was going to die," Bonnell said. "I was more sick than I'd ever been in my whole life, ever before or ever since. It just drained me, and the next day, I think we were in Chicago and I had trouble picking the bat up, I was so weak. I was just drained from the whole experience."

The next morning, one of the coaches took Bonnell and Murphy out to breakfast and, unaware that Bonnell had been hospitalized, accused them of spending their money on tithing—the custom of giving 10 percent of a member's income to the church—"instead of paying for good food."

"That was a time when I was flabbergasted by what he said," Bonnell said. "I told him it was the most ridiculous thing I had ever heard in my entire life, we wouldn't give our money to the church and not eat."

In the LDS church, the doctrine of foreordination is important for the way it ties individuals to God—they are, basically, selected to fulfill certain callings—but unlike the concept of predestination, individuals have the ability to choose whether they answer that calling.

Dale Murphy had a choice.

Selected by the Braves with the fifth overall pick in the 1974 draft, the Portland product had signed a letter of intent to attend Arizona State. He didn't believe he'd be taken that early, but when scout Bill Wight came to his home and started negotiating a contract, "I didn't know how it all worked . . . we had no idea what to ask for," Murphy said. "We were just flying by the seat of our pants, my dad and I."

They settled on a little over $50,000, as Murphy remembers, his parents asking him what he wanted to do next.

"I guess I'll go for it," he told them. "I guess I'll try this professional baseball thing."

That decision would lead him to Bonnell and becoming Mormon—so great was their impact on each other that Bonnell named a son after Murphy, while Murphy gave one of his children the middle name Bonnell. It led him to going to BYU and meeting Nancy, and it would ultimately set the stage for a new path in a career that he was afraid was blowing up before his eyes.

"There's no question that the decision to sign with the Braves impacted my life in so many, many ways on and off the field," Murphy said. "I look as far as baseball is concerned and I don't think I could have gone through what I went through with other organizations."

*   *   *   *

He couldn't throw. The 6-foot-4, 210-pound catcher went into spring training in 1977 facing comparisons like this from the (Kingsport) *Daily News*: "they speak of Murphy as another Johnny Bench, and they don't mean he's another .260 hitter. They refer to his arm." But it was that arm that was turning against him. Murphy was unable to make the most basic of plays from behind the plate, developing a mental block when it came to throwing out runners.

"I wanted to quit," he said.

During one of the final days of spring, he came within inches of nailing Rick Camp. The right-hander hit the dirt in order to give Murphy extra room, but instead he threw it right at him. Murphy hit umpires. In Triple A he hit his own pitcher in the butt while he was laying on the grass.

"It made me happy because he kept throwing them in the air to center field and I'd throw them out at third base, so it increased my stock," Bonnell said. "That's just a joke . . . but it did happen a couple of times."

Bonnell believes that throwing phobia was a result of the hype being heaped upon Murphy, who at the time had appeared in just nineteen major-league games.

"We went to spring training and the reporters were flocking around him, and that really affects a young guy, that kind of attention gets plastered on him when he hasn't really proven himself yet and suddenly he's thrust into that kind of spotlight," Bonnell said. "I think that was kind of wearing on him a little bit."

He remembers it coming to a head during a game against the Reds as a batter got on base and attempted to steal second. Murphy's throw was off and the ball sailed into the outfield, and then, on the next pitch, the runner took off for third base and, again, Murphy's throw went into the outfield.

Braves manager Dave Bristol had seen enough, pulling Murphy from the game.

"He just went and got him like he was changing a pitcher and he changed the catcher," Bonnell said.

Bonnell wouldn't see Murphy the rest of the game, and after he had finished showering and returned to his locker—being number 2, his locker was next to Murphy's—he noticed Murphy's street clothes were s till there.

"I'm going 'Where is he?'" Bonnell said.

Eventually, Murphy walked in, his body caked with dirt, that mixed with sweat, looked more like mud.

"Where in the heck have you been?" Bonnell asked him.

"Well, they took me over on the minor-league fields and had me throwing to the bases," Murphy responded.

"For two hours?" asked Bonnell.

"That just killed him and from then on he couldn't throw," Bonnell recalls. "That's what took him out of the catching game."

Murphy was sent down to Triple-A Richmond and shortly after that demotion, he remembers a particularly bad day throwing. He was paid a visit by Paul Snyder, a former Braves first baseman and outfielder who that year had taken over the reins of the organization's farm system.

"He basically gave me kind of a talk, 'Hey, you know, you've got your health,' kind of a count-your-blessings kind of thing when I didn't think I had any blessings," Murphy said. "I was like 'What am I going to do?'"

Murphy would get a September call-up to Atlanta, but proceeded to commit six errors in seventeen games behind the plate and picked off runners just 17 percent of the time, 18 percent lower than the league average.

"I threw some guys out, I did. It was just not consistent enough, obviously," Murphy said. "I could throw it back to the pitcher, but not well enough to where, 'Okay, he's going to be our everyday catcher.'"

His potential at the plate too great to ignore—Murphy hit .305 with 90 RBIs and 22 home runs in 466 at-bats in Triple A in '77—the Braves tried him at first base, and in 1978, his first full season in the majors, he started 125 games at the position. Murphy led the league with 20 errors, and his .984 fielding percentage was nineteenth among all first basemen. A year later, he had 15 errors at first and his fielding percentage slipped to .980, all while playing just 75 games. He played another 27 games behind the plate, where his caught-stealing percentage was at 16, while the league average was 34.

"I just had no idea what to do," Murphy said.

Luckily, Bobby Cox did.

That offseason, after he and Nancy were married, Murphy received a phone call from the Braves' new manager, who was months removed from being a member of Billy Martin's staff with the world champion Yankees. He and minor-league coach Bobby Dews had come with an idea.

"Murphy, what do you think?" Cox asked him. "What about the outfield."

"I'm game," Murphy said. "I'll go for it."

Finally, he had found a home.

In 1980, at 24 years old, Murphy played 154 games in the outfield—129 of them in center—and earned the first of his All-Star Game nods. His .985 fielding percentage was fourth among all center fielders, and while he admits he missed his share of cutoff men, his defense was no longer the issue it once was.

"My throwing, I wasn't all that accurate out there, but you get in the outfield, you're relaxed, your throws are longer," Murphy said. "I was like, 'Dang, this is great. I'm really contributing defensively. What a shock?' And it helped me offensively. It kind of settled me down. I had a position. I felt like I could stay."

Most stunning of all—considering his issues behind the plate and at first—was that 1982, Murphy's third season in the outfield, was the first of five consecutive Gold Glove–winning seasons.

"To think a couple of years before that, that I was going to be around? I didn't really see it," Murphy said. "I didn't really see it. But I'm glad they did."

In 1982 and 1983, Murphy became the first Brave and the fourth NL player to win back-to-back MVP awards as he hit a combined .291/.386/.523 with 72 home runs and 230 RBIs (he led the majors in both years with 109 in 1982 and 121 the following season). Murphy's '83 campaign saw him hit 36 homers and swipe 30 bases, marking the franchise's first 30/30 season since Hank Aaron in 1963.

From 1982 to 1985 he was the MLB leader in games played (641)—never missing a game for four straight years—homers (145), and runs created (503), and along with those MVP awards, finished ninth in voting in '84 and seventh in '85.

"You can put him in a class with a Mays and an Aaron because he can beat you with his glove, and he can beat you with a home run," said former Braves manager Joe Torre.

Said comedian Jeff Foxworthy, an Atlanta native and lifelong Braves fan, "For the Braves fans back then, there were some bad teams. . . . This would be me calling home from the road, because I'm doing shows every night at comedy clubs, and I would call my wife:

'Braves win?'

'No.'

'What did Murph do?'

"So if Murph went three-for-four that was your consolation prize."

But as great as Murphy was, he also experienced a dramatic decline.

After hitting .295/.417/.580—that on-base percentage was a career-best—in 1987, his average plummeted to .228 over his next two-plus seasons in Atlanta and he hit a combined 68 home runs in 1,515 plate appearances. That's a homer every 22.2 at-bats, compared to 16.4 in his prime.

Trade rumors heated up. In the winter of 1988, the Mets began making a play for Murphy, with the Braves looking at a package of Lenny Dykstra, Howard Johnson, Keith Miller, and David West in return. Meanwhile, the Padres dangled Sandy Alomar Jr., John Kruk, and Greg Harris.

The Braves were unable to pull the trigger, though they didn't get much help from the potential haul they were seeking from New York.

In the clubhouse before they were to take infield, Johnson told Dykstra that a Braves scout was in town to see them.

"They're like, 'Man, I don't want to go to Atlanta. I don't want to go,'" Murphy recounted.

Reluctantly, they went out onto the field. Johnson took the first groundball that came his way at third base, launched it over the first baseman's head, and then grabbed his throwing arm, feigning injury as he walked back into the clubhouse.

"(He was) trying to fake the scouts out like he was hurt," Murphy said, laughing.

Murphy had veto power, having spent more than ten years with the Braves, but said he would "keep all my options open." But the talk had an unexpected effect on him. Two seasons removed from being an All-Star, he wondered if a change of scenery could be what he needed to launch a career resurgence.

"It would kind of get my adrenaline going a little bit, to be honest with you. I don't think I really said that before," he revealed. "I was just like 'Okay, what would it be like to play in New York? Gee whiz, that would be really interesting. That could be exciting. That could be fun. Maybe that could get me going again, because we're not doing anything. I'm struggling.'"

It wasn't just Murphy that was in a bad place. The Braves were coming off a 106-loss season and had dropped at least 89 in each of the previous four years. The upcoming 1989 campaign would see them drop 97, and they'd do the same in 1990.

"I was struggling and the team was struggling and I could sense that," he said.

Dale and Nancy talked and they had come to a difficult decision. He never considered himself an assertive person, but Murphy walked into the office of Cox, who at the time was serving as both the general manager and manager, and with free agency looming after the 1990 season, offered a solution that could help him and the only team he'd ever played for.

"I think it's time to go. I'm going to go next year," he told Cox. "You know, if there's a trade that looks like another team [will add to my existing contract], I'll do that instead of going out on the market."

They found a willing partner in the Phillies, and on August 3, 1990, Philadelphia landed Murphy for pitcher Jeff Parrett and two players to be named later (Victor Rosario and Jim Vatcher). Philadelphia would sign Murphy to a two-year, $5 million extension.

"The Philly thing came up and we talked to Bruce Church, our agent, and he said 'They're willing to add a year to your contract, same salary,' and Philly looked like they had some things percolating in that organization," Murphy said. "I was like, 'Well, there's nothing more different than Atlanta than Philly.' It kind of was like New York and it could energize me and it did."

Dale Murphy, the centerpiece of the Braves in the TBS era for more than a decade, was gone. A figure that had become larger than life, seen wielding a light saber in a 1980s Nike poster, was no longer a Brave. The man who influenced a generation by penning a weekly advice column for children in both the *Atlanta Journal* and *Constitution* called "Ask Dale Murphy," had left town.

Braves fans, expectedly, were hit hard.

"I'm not ashamed of this and I told Dale this when I finally met him," said Foxworthy. "The day I got on the plane, and I stop and buy the paper, and I open it up and it said Murph was traded, I had to hold the paper up because I was crying. I had tears rolling down my face. I'm like 'No, not Murph. No.'"

To this day, Murphy has to go through the story with fans who don't realize he was the one who requested the trade, which ultimately opened the door for David Justice, a two-time All-Star for the Braves and the 1990 Rookie of the Year.

"When it did happen, man, I didn't realize the emotions and I don't realize them much until now fans talk to me all these years later," Murphy said. "That story about Jeff (Foxworthy) and other fans . . . It just chokes you up that you were a part of their lives, that important part of their lives. It's something you don't realize at the time and it's something that I don't think retired players, that what we're going through or what we mean to people as a professional ball player and you're on their team and what it means to people.

"But boy, when you get retired and you get away from it for a few decades, you're like, 'That was really a lucky time for all of us.' Sometimes when you're young you just don't understand it. I tried to understand it but I understand it a lot more [now]."

*   *   *   *

The Baseball Project penned an ode to Dale Murphy's Hall of Fame worthiness with the song "To the Veterans Committee," because Murphy's road to Cooperstown technically now goes through the Expansion Era Committee.

After fifteen years, Murphy failed in his final chance on the Hall of Fame ballot in 2013. Needing to appear on 75 percent of the ballots of the Baseball Writers Association of America (BBWAA), he was at 18.6 percent that last season, peaking at 23.2 in 2000, his second year of eligibility.

His eight children launched a campaign of their own in that final push. Chad, a PhD candidate in Organizational Behavior at Penn State, wrote a letter to voters, while Taylor launched an online petition that would generate more than 6,000 supporters, including Larry King, Justin Verlander, and Dick Vitale.

Tyson, an artist who works for Blizzard Entertainment, created a cartoon, and Madison, the only daughter, wrote a piece entitled "My Dad Is a Super Hero." The other children (Jake, McKay, Shawn, and Travis) got involved by taking part in interviews.

"It's been like Christmas and Father's Day times a hundred," Murphy told the *Desert News*. "It's just an emotional and tender feeling of what the kids have put together in their efforts. They've just gone the extra mile for me. 'Thanks' does not sound like the adequate word."

He also received an assist from Braves president John Schuerholz, who sent out a letter of his own to voters asking them to take a closer look at Murphy's resume.

"The Atlanta Braves organization is extremely proud of Dale's outstanding accomplishments during an extraordinary eighteen-year major league career, fifteen of which were spent with the Braves," he wrote.

"Not only on the field, but off the field as well, Dale represented himself and the city of Atlanta with the class and professionalism consistent with the ideals of Major League Baseball and the Hall of Fame in Cooperstown. Even today, he continues to be one of our game's greatest ambassadors."

But he fell short, and Murphy now stands with Roger Maris as the only two-time MVPs who have yet to be enshrined in Cooperstown. But there is more than a shred of hope for Murphy: the Eras Committee.

In all its forms, it has elected ninety-six players over the years.

Previously, living HOF members made up a single electoral body: the Veterans Committee. But since 2010 it has been broken down into three subgroups responsible for three time periods: Pre-Integration Era (1871–1946), Golden Era (1947–72), and Expansion Era (1973 on). Made up of twelve HOFers—including contemporaries Johnny Bench, Eddie Murray, Jim Palmer, Tony Perez, Ryne Sandberg, and Ozzie Smith—executives, historians, and media members, Murphy's hopes now reside with the sixteen-member Expansion Era Committee, which meets every three years.

A Historical Review Committee, appointed by the BBWAA, puts forth a group of twelve candidates each year. The Expansion Era's next vote comes at the 2016 Winter Meetings for induction in 2017.

"I thought I'd get more support over the course of the fifteen years," Murphy told MLB.com in 2013. "I got a significant percentage boost. I'm very thankful for that. It's really been a great experience the past month. The support from fans and the media, it all brought back great memories. I'm very thankful for that. I have no complaints.

"If I was sitting here at 65 percent, I'd say I'm disappointed. I can't lie to you. But it's been a great experience. It really has been. I feel very lucky to have been on the ballot for fifteen years."

Foreordination. The outcome of that choice to become an Atlanta Brave spawned everything after it and shaped the man. Murphy's career ended in Colorado in 1993, a shell of who he once was, a player now making the league minimum and posting an average (.143) that would be the lowest of his eighteen years in the majors.

But the lasting image is Murphy in Atlanta, and his continued impact on the Braves and the love affair with fans is undeniable. His number-3 jersey is still spotted throughout the Turner Field stands, the image of that Power Alley poster gracing T-shirts.

"I grew up in a Braves uniform, started at eighteen, and you know, raised my family with Nancy in a Braves uniform," Murphy said. "It's one of the main parts of who we are, both me and Nancy, and so many things—good memories, good people, growing experiences—happened in my time in a Braves uniform. It means a lot. It's a cherished part of my life."

Chapter Four

The Dawn of a Dynasty

They boarded the plane for the four-hour flight back to Atlanta from Los Angeles for the 1991 All-Star break, staring down a deficit in the National League West that had grown to nine and a half games after dropping two of three to the division-leading Dodgers in Chavez Ravine.

It was there, some 40,000 feet in the air, that the Braves' season changed.

"Nobody sat down," said third baseman Terry Pendleton. "Everybody stood up the whole time, talking about what we could do, how good we could be and how we hadn't played well in the first half and how much better of a team we could be if we played the way we were capable of playing."

One season removed from finishing last in the West—26 games behind the eventual World Series champion Reds—there was inexplicably a sense of possibility. That was what drove Pendleton to Atlanta in the first place.

Following the 1990 season, the Los Angeles native had packed up everything and moved back home after spending seven seasons with the Cardinals, expecting that he'd now be a Dodger. But the Dodgers didn't pursue him, and neither did twenty-four other teams, as only the Braves and Yankees showed interest in the 31-year-old two-time Gold Glove winner who had never hit higher than .286 in a single season.

"[The Yankees] pursued very hard, but the Braves didn't stop pursuing," Pendleton said. "[General manager] John Schuerholz didn't stop pursuing."

New York was offering more money—about $2.55 million annually—but he ultimately signed with Atlanta for four years because of what he had seen when he took on the Braves.

Pendleton had faced the likes of Tom Glavine and John Smoltz, who were 25 and 24, respectively. He realized that with such pitching, combined with a core of position players that included shortstop Jeff Blauser, outfielder and reigning Rookie of the Year David Justice, and second baseman Mark Lemke (all of whom were 25), as well as outfielder Ron Gant (26), Atlanta had long-term potential.

"If they played defense and caught the ball and had a way to score a few runs here and there, they had a chance to do something special," Pendleton said.

He signed on December 3, 1990, and later that month the Braves added two more veteran free agents in former Pirates shortstop Rafael Belliard and first baseman Sid Bream. The two were coming off a trip to the NLCS in Pittsburgh, and with Pendleton having played in the World Series with the Cardinals in 1985 and 1987, first-year GM Schuerholz's plan was becoming clear.

He was, in essence, protecting the youth movement that general manager-turned-manager (again) Bobby Cox jump-started, but Schuerholz's reclamation project went beyond the on-field product. He installed a coat-and-tie dress code in the front office and hired away the Royals groundskeeper, Ed Mangan, to revamp a field considered among the worst in the majors.

"It was my job to find those complementary players—Terry Pendleton, Rafael Belliard, Sid Bream, and in spring training, Otis Nixon, in Year One—to utilize the strengths that were already in place, which was mainly young pitching," said Schuerholz, who had joined the Braves in October from Kansas City, "and supplement that with solid defensive players and leaders, people who had been in winning circumstances most of their careers, and that's what we did."

In all, he signed six free agents to the tune of $30 million for that season, which included outfielder Deion Sanders, who would remain with the team until July 31—he was batting .198—to return to his other life as the Falcons cornerback.

Sanders would famously combine those two worlds on September 25 when he practiced with the Falcons in Suwanee, Georgia, then caught a ride in an Atlanta news helicopter to a parking lot near the state capitol near Atlanta–Fulton County Stadium. He served as a pinch runner in both games of a doubleheader with the Reds, returning from a 51-game absence.

Asked if Sanders fit in with the Braves' corporate/team-centric approach in his four seasons, Schuerholz replied, "No. [He] didn't. But he was an absolutely great talent. . . . I've been in baseball fifty years. Bo Jackson number one, Deion Sanders number two that I've been with [who were just] dynamic physical-ability packages. Both obviously multi-sport talents, Pro Bowlers in their other sport, could have been All-Stars every year in our sport."

Sanders has had a lasting legacy in Atlanta, though, with his very presence in a Braves uniform spawning one of the franchise's most recognizable traditions: the tomahawk chop.

When the Florida State product would go to the plate in spring training in the Sunshine State, Seminoles fans in attendance broke into the school's war chant and chop. It followed Sanders and the Braves back to Atlanta, and with the help of Schuerholz, who urged the Atlanta–Fulton County Stadium organist to play the chant music when the Braves rallied, it has become a staple.

That spring Cox allowed the veterans to lead a closed-door meeting in which they laid out what they thought the team was capable of despite the fact that no NL team had ever gone from last place one year to first the next.

They were competitive, going 8–10 in April and 17–9 in May to climb within a half game of the first-place Dodgers, but a 12–17 June combined with that pre–All-Star Game July in which they went 2–4 left the Braves facing a nearly double-digit hole heading into the second half of the season.

"The first half it was like an unsure thing: 'Can we play? Is our team this good?'" Pendleton said of the young players. "We had veteran players like myself, Sid Bream, Otis Nixon, Rafael Belliard, Mike Keith. We had some veteran players that knew what it took to win and knew how good we could be. But the young kids, I don't think they really understood that."

They would.

The Braves came back after the break against the Cardinals on July 11, a crowd of 17,060 marking the seventeenth time in 41 home games that they had played in front of less than 20,000 fans.

Left-hander Steve Avery was dominant, holding St. Louis to just two hits over 7⅓ scoreless innings with five strikeouts and one walk, while Pendleton and Lonnie Smith had two hits each in a 4–1 win. Atlanta would open the season's second half with four straight wins and claim 14 of 20 to move within four and a half of the Dodgers.

Pendleton started to see a change in the team. He would often sit in the dugout, to the outsider simply relaxing before the game, but he was also monitoring the evolving body language of the team's young core.

"We started the second half doing what we were capable of doing and to see those young kids walk out onto the field every day after that, it didn't matter where it was, you watched them," he said. "I was watching their attitudes and actions and how they walked out on anybody's field to start batting practice knowing they were going to kick their rear end. They had that cocky confidence about them."

The youth was a factor, but so too was the defense.

After finishing last in the majors with 158 fielding errors in '90, the Braves committed 138 in '91, an improvement that had much to do with the play of Pendleton and Belliard and Nixon. They were the team's leaders in TotalZone—a defensive statistic designed and calculated by BaseballProjection.com's Sean Smith using play-by-play data—with seven via Pendleton, while Belliard had three and Nixon two. Only three other Atlanta players (Bream, Tommy Gregg, and Keith Mitchell with one apiece) were in the positive.

"Did we need to improve the defense?" starter Charlie Leibrandt told the *Los Angeles Times*. "No question about it. We needed to and we did."

The Braves would go 19–11 in August, including winning five of the last six to lead the West by as many as two games. But over the next twenty-three days Atlanta and Los Angeles would be separated by no more than a game and a half, with the Braves up just seven times. Confounding things for both sides, they split their final six meetings, with Atlanta winning two of three in Georgia and the Dodgers taking two of three in California.

That stretch would see the Braves rattle off a seven-game winning streak that included something never before seen at Atlanta–Fulton County Stadium: a no-hitter.

A stopgap starter who was thrust into the rotation after Armando Reynoso didn't work out, Kent Mercker shut down the Padres for six innings on September 11 before rookie Mark Wohlers took over for two innings and Alejandro Pena finished things off. It was the first ever combined no-hitter in NL history.

And it came with controversy.

With San Diego down to their last out, Darrin Jackson hit an 0–2 pitch between third base and shortstop, and as Pendleton moved toward the ball he backed away and it glanced off Belliard. Despite never touching the ball, official scorer Mark Frederickson ruled it an error on Pendleton.

"Pendleton could have had the ball," Frederickson told reporters. "He let it go by. Pendleton committed on the ball, and if he would have gone ahead and made the play, he would have thrown him out."

Pena would then get Tony Gwynn, who at the time was the league's leading hitter, to fly out to left to secure the second no-no in Braves history. The first came via Phil Niekro on August 5, 1973—also against the Pirates.

"I lost it in the lights. I missed it," Pendleton told the *Atlanta Journal-Constitution.* "Thank you, Mr. Scorer, for that E-5."

Consider it luck being on their side, but a comeback victory in Cincinnati on October 1 would further spark "team of destiny" talk.

"I don't believe in that stuff," Cox would say. "I believe in good players."

Down 6–0 after the first inning, as the Reds teed off on Charlie Leibrandt—punctuated by a Joe Oliver grand slam—Atlanta rebounded and combined with Pete Smith, Mike Bielecki, Mike Stanton, and Pena to allow just three hits over the last eight innings.

The Braves' bats managed to cut the lead to 6–5 heading into the ninth, getting to Jose Rijo (who came in with a 9–0 home record and a NL-best 2.32 ERA), before a ninth inning in which Cincinnati native Justice hit a two-run home run off Rob Dibble. It kept the Braves one game behind Los Angeles with four games to play.

All the while, the city of Atlanta was getting swept up in the rise of a team that before 1991 hadn't had a winning month in nearly two years.

After averaging 23,935 fans during the first half of the season, the Braves would increase to 31,356 in the second half and over 35,000 in the final two homestands of the season.

"That was a thrill for me, and then to see the stadium fill up after that," Pendleton said. "You know, that's all people talked about. You turned on the news and that's all people talked about. It was amazing, and then you go to other cities and that's all they talked about was the way the Atlanta Braves were playing baseball and the young talent that they had."

Comedian Jeff Foxworthy recalls being in Atlanta for the last home game vs. the Dodgers on September 15 as Sid Bream hit a first-inning grand slam, propelling the Braves to a 9–1 win that gave them a game and a half edge in the division. Foxworthy was a longtime fan who was there when a few thousand fans would come to games—"I can remember going to games in the late '70s and early '80s and somebody would hit a foul ball and you'd look at your buddy and go 'Do you want it or can I get it?'" he said. "I mean, there was like nobody there. There were some bad teams—it was a stunning change.

"That stadium was rocking and people were just so hungry for it and you're driving downtown and people are standing on the street corner doing the chop," he said. "It was like a fever in Atlanta."

Schuerholz would be approached while speaking at Rotary Clubs and Kiwanis Clubs and heard from excited fans. He'd get it at restaurants or from the letters he received from across the country—underscoring the team's reach via TBS—from retirement homes, longtime followers referring to the Braves as "my boys."

"It just was so, almost spiritual. It was that way," he said. "That's how it felt, a spiritual experience for Braves fans, and I was a part of that."

For those players who were a part of the previous struggles, and especially those that were products of Atlanta's farm system, the change took on an even greater meaning.

"I think that year was probably the most special for the guys that came up through the organization, Ron Gant, myself, David Justice, Jeff Blauser, all those guys that came through, Tommy [Glavine], of course," said Lemke. "We all came up together and we all started out on kind of some very poor teams, just to see that transition and to be part of it was just the most incredible thing.

"To see the emotion and just the excitement of the fans and the city . . . I mean, it was overwhelming. It really was. The hair on your arms would stand up. I've never played in games with that amount of electricity going as we had back in 1991 at old Fulton County Stadium."

On October 5, the next to the last day of the season, the Braves' improbable rebound was near completion and Chip Caray saw an opportunity to honor one of the voices that had been there through those difficult seasons.

The game was being broadcast nationally on CBS, and Caray was on the Braves Radio Network call with Pete Van Wieren. He was filling in for his dad, Skip, who was broadcasting an NFL game on TNT, and Dave O'Brien, who was off doing a Georgia football game for WSB-AM.

The Braves' radio personalities would typically rotate after a set amount of innings, and in this case, Caray was in line to take the eighth and ninth. But as the ninth started and the team could do its part to deliver the division title, Caray took Van Wieren—who had been calling games since 1976—by surprise.

"So I just came back from break and, I don't remember the exact words, but I said something like 'It's been ten years since Ernie Johnson, my dad Skip Caray, and Pete Van Wieren, Darrel Chaney had a chance to call a winner. The Braves are three outs from the Western Division title, and here with the play-by-play is Pete Van Wieren,'" said Caray, who currently calls games for FOX Sports South and FOX Sports Southeast. "He didn't know I was going to do it. I took off my headset and got up and walked out of the booth."

With Van Wieren delivering the backdrop, the Braves beat the Astros 5–2, but it wasn't until Eddie Murray flied out in the ninth in San Francisco, ending the Dodgers' hopes, that Atlanta clinched. The Braves, who had been standing in the infield watching, celebrated while 44,994 home fans chopped and James Brown's "I Feel Good" played through the public-address system.

"In spring training, no one picked us to have such a good team. But we knew in that clubhouse that we had a good team and it was just a matter of how well we matured and gelled together," Justice would say.

Three time zones away, dejected Los Angeles outfielder Darryl Strawberry saw things a different way: "You look at some of the teams they've played, some of the teams they played didn't care too much about winning," he told reporters. "Whoever played us always cared about winning and when they played Atlanta, it was a different story."

Local TV cameras captured Sanders giving Avery—who allowed two runs in eight innings of the series opener with Houston that gave the Braves a one-game lead over the Dodgers—a piggyback ride. "Avery carried us the whole series, so I'm going to carry him now," Sanders said.

The arrival of Pendleton and the veterans was crucial, as the third baseman was the NL's Most Valuable Player as he won a batting title with a .319 average to go along with 22 home runs and 86 RBIs, and Gant had a 30–30 season with 32 homers and 34 steals and drove in 105 runs. But it was the starting pitching that fueled the 1991 run and the thirteen division titles that would follow.

Glavine emerged as an ace, winning his first Cy Young at age 25 as he went 20–11 with a 2.55 ERA, while Avery, twenty-one, went from a 3–11 rookie season to an 18–8 record and 3.38 ERA. Leibrandt—who at 34 was nine years older than any other Braves primary starter—won 15 games.

But if the miraculous story of the Braves' season was embodied by one player, it was the other piece of that rotation: John Smoltz.

"He has to erase the whole first half from his mind," Cox said July 6 as Smoltz gave up five runs (and didn't make it through the second inning) to fall to 2–11, a major-league high for losses. "There's really not much I can say."

Plagued by a lack of control, the debate raged whether the right-hander should move to the bullpen or be demoted to the minors.

Cox did neither.

"Bobby Cox did not take him out of the rotation and said he was not going to take him out of the rotation because he said it was the best 2–11 record he had seen in a long time," said pitching coach Leo Mazzone.

It was a sentiment that went beyond Cox, as the front office had high hopes for the 24-year-old, who was in his third full season in the majors and the year before won 14 games.

"Even though he was 2–11 he was intense, aggressive, confident," Schuerholz said. "You knew this guy was going to be a success somewhere down the line."

When Atlanta beat Houston in that win that would clinch the division, it was with Smoltz on the mound. He allowed just two runs over nine innings, and as Andújar Cedeño popped out to Justice to end the game, Smoltz held his arms skyward as catcher Greg Olson embraced him.

"I can't say enough about my teammates and Bobby Cox for giving me all the confidence in the world after the first half and sticking with me," Smoltz told CBS afterward.

It was an exclamation point of a performance after he went 12–2 following the All-Star break, with a 2.63 ERA in 18 starts, 78 strikeouts, and 33 walks in 123⅓ innings— and at the center of it was a man in red.

Sports psychologist Dr. Jack Llewellyn had been working with baseball players since 1976 with a focus on positive visualization. In the case of Smoltz, Llewellyn's tactic was simple: He whittled six hours of tape down to six pitches—three to right-handed batters; three to left—a fastball, curveball, and slider that amounted to two and a half minutes of highlights of Smoltz at his best.

"It was like I had a cupful of emotions," Smoltz told the *Baltimore Sun* of his first-half problems. "Every time there was an error or a bad pitch, I'd let everything spill out. Inside, it was tearing me up. I'm no dummy. I know

I'm a major part of this team. But I don't plan on ever going through anything like that again."

With Llewellyn's help when things weren't going right on the mound, Smoltz could mentally put himself back into the proper place by remembering those moments of success.

Remember the good and forget the bad.

"The important thing is recovery speed," Llewellyn told the *Sun*. "My position is what separates good pitchers from great pitchers is speed of recovery."

If Smoltz needed another visual reminder for that recovery, Llewellyn could be seen sitting behind home plate during each of Smoltz's starts after the break. He would wear red to make him easier to spot—not that Smoltz needed the further cue.

"The idea was for a focusing technique, and I can honestly say that I never, ever saw it, never looked in the stands," Smoltz said years later. "It became a good-luck thing with Jack."

After an Atlanta-record 94 wins in the regular season, including a 55–28 mark in the second half and an awards haul that included Glavine's Cy Young, Pendleton's MVP, and Cox being named Manager of the Year, baseball seemed to belong to the Braves.

"We haven't been able to win the last few years and for this thing to come together and the young pitchers do the job that they've done, it's really something great," Gant said after the division-clincher. "I feel like we're going to win everything . . . the World Series, playoffs, everything."

It continued during a seven-game win over the Pirates in the NLCS that was kicked off by Avery, bringing an end to a seven-game playoff losing streak that began in 1969.

Avery started Game Two, becoming the youngest pitcher to do so since 20-year-old Bret Saberhagen for the Royals in 1984, and would throw 8⅓ shutout innings in a

1–0 win in Three Rivers Stadium. With the Pirates leading the series 3–2, Avery followed with eight more scoreless innings in Game Six to force a Game Seven, en route to winning series MVP with 17 strikeouts and an NLCS record of 16⅓ innings without allowing a run.

In Avery's second outing, the Braves outfield had one putout, tying an LCS record.

"Usually, I get balls because guys fall behind Avery and hit them to right field," Justice told the *Journal-Constitution*. "But I was in right field and I was just there. I should have had a Walkman."

In a season of firsts, the Braves became the only NL team to claim the final two games of the championship series and take the pennant. Brian Hunter hit a home run and had three RBIs, while Smoltz threw a complete-game shutout in a 4–0 victory in Game Seven.

He allowed six hits, one by Barry Bonds and zero from Andy Van Slyke as Atlanta's arms held them to averages of .148 and .160, respectively.

"There is nothing better than winning; and this is the greatest year of my life, so far," Smoltz said following the win.

The Braves weren't supposed to be in the World Series, and neither were the American League champs.

The Twins finished 29 games back in the AL West in 1990, and like Atlanta, had made an improbable run to a pennant, dumping the Blue Jays in five games in the ALCS.

They would wage what ESPN tabbed as the greatest of all World Series in their 100th anniversary countdown. It featured three extra-inning affairs—Game Three went 12 innings, Game Six lasted 11, and Game Seven ended in 10—and aside from the Twins' 5–2 victory in the opener and the Braves' 14–5 rout in Game Five, the other five games were decided by one run.

Minnesota jumped out to a 2–0 series lead, with that second win aided by a moment that's still a sore subject.

With two outs in the third inning, Gant ripped a single to left field as Lonnie Smith—who reached on an error—ran to third base. The ball was overthrown by Dan Gladden, and Twins starter Kevin Tapani fielded it between third and home. The pitcher quickly fired to first base and Gant moved back to the bag, where Kent Hrbek—Minnesota's 235-pound first baseman—lifted Gant's right leg up with his glove hand and propelled him off the base. Drew Coble called him out, ending the inning, and the Braves would go on to fall 3–2.

"He definitely tried to push me off the base," Gant said following the loss. "I don't understand the call."

The Twins celebrated that moment during the twentieth anniversary of the championship with a bobblehead of Gant and Hrbek entangled. Braves director of public relations Beth Marshall told the *Star-Tribune* "We begrudgingly gave our approval [to the design] because, although it wasn't a great moment in Braves history, it was for the Twins!"

When Atlanta punched its ticket to the Series, Foxworthy received a call from his friend, Mike. He had two tickets for Game Three, behind the Braves dugout. The problem was that not only had Foxworthy moved to Los Angeles the year before at the urging of his wife, who'd told him he'd need to move to try to make it as a comedian, but she was due with the couple's first baby that week.

"Oh, dude, I can't do it," Foxworthy told his friend, "because if I get on a plane and she goes into labor I can't turn around fast enough."

He mentioned the call to his wife, Pamela, who said "You took it, didn't you?"

"No," Foxworthy replied. "You know if you go into labor, I can't get back."

"We'll have another kid," she told him. "The Braves may never go to the World Series again."

He didn't miss the birth of his daughter, Jordan, or an epic game that lasted a then-record four hours and four minutes. Atlanta won in 12 innings as Lemke poked a base hit to left field, allowing Justice to beat Gladden's throw for a 5–4 win. Lemke would again play the hero in Game Four—and thanks to Game Three ending after midnight, became the only player to win two World Series games in the same day—getting around a throw to the plate from Jerry Willard as the Braves won 3–2.

Lemke, who at the time was a career .225 hitter, batted .417 in the series.

Momentum on their side, Atlanta racked up 17 hits in the Game Five rout, including a two-run homer from Justice and solo shots from Smith and Hunter, while Gant and Olson had three hits apiece. But the Twins would claim Game Six 1–0 behind Kirby Puckett.

The future Hall of Famer stole the show with a leaping grab at the wall to rob Gant of a run-scoring extra-base hit and went 3-for-4 at the plate with an RBI triple, a sac fly that drove in a run, a single, and finally, the walk-off home run off Leibrandt in the eleventh. That Cox had gone to Leibrandt, who had a 9.00 ERA from lasting four innings in Game One, to face the red-hot Puckett, was a head-scratching hot topic.

But Leibrandt had struck Puckett out twice in the opener, and that was what Cox was leaning on.

"Pretty stupid if we are resistant in bringing in a fifteen-game winner," Cox said that night. "We had handled Puckett in the first game, he [Leibrandt] just got a change-up up."

Jack Morris and Smoltz—a Michigan native and former Tigers prospect who idolized the Twins righty—went toe-to-toe in Game Seven, with Smoltz throwing 7⅓ scoreless innings before the disgusted starter flipped the ball to Cox, who turned things over to the bullpen.

"I wanted to stay out there and, to be honest, it surprised me a little to come out of there," Smoltz said later.

A photo was taken afterward of Smoltz, sitting alone in the visiting dugout as Minnesota celebrated. Gene Larkin had dropped a hit into left field in the 10th inning off Pena, scoring Gladden, who jumped onto home plate before he was mobbed by teammates.

"I've never seen John lose," Llewellyn would say.

Worst-to-First indeed ended in a ticker-tape parade, just not for a title. An estimated 750,000-plus flooded downtown to cheer as the Braves made their way down Peachtree Street. It included sixteen marching bands and a baseball-bat drill team.

"I've been in parades before in New York," Cox, who played with the Yankees, told the *Journal-Constitution.* "But I've never seen anything like this. Nothing."

The Braves had created a frenzy in a city that had waited decades for it.

"Everything about that year was just magical," Glavine said. "It was crazy at times. You still see those images of people at the time doing the tomahawk chop and you get goose bumps. That was just a special, special year; just didn't end right. It wasn't the storybook ending."

No, but it was just the beginning.

Chapter Five

"Here Comes Bream! Here's the Throw to the Plate . . ."

To one legion of fans it's known as The Slide; to another, it's the Bream Curse. No matter the nomenclature, more than twenty years later, Sid Bream still hears about it, and living in metro Pittsburgh—where he works in real estate—he gets an earful from one impassioned fan base impacted by Game Seven of the 1992 National League Championship Series.

"Any day I'm in the public, I hear it. I still hear it even though the Pirates have started to win," he said.

Not that he's complaining.

Whether he's deemed hero or villain, when Bream's surgically-repaired (five times over) knees catapulted the

Braves to their second straight World Series, it gave the first baseman's career a life it likely never would have had on its own.

"As Bill Buckner's ball went through his legs, that's what I'm known for. Other than that, I really and truly believe I would have gone into obscurity in a sense," Bream said. "You know, not a franchise player—but that one play has stayed alive."

Atlanta was down 2–0 in the bottom of the ninth with Terry Pendleton on third base and David Justice on first when the 31-year-old Bream dug his left foot into the batter's box before stepping in.

He looked across at Pirates starter Doug Drabek—two men with a past.

Two years before that night at Atlanta–Fulton County Stadium, Bream was a Pirate. He had every intention of staying one too, when he entered free agency after the 1990 season, but contract negotiations hit an impasse. Despite general manager Larry Doughty calling Bream the "glue" that held the team together, and his agreeing to take Pittsburgh's last offer of $4.5 million for three years—the Braves were offering $5.6 million over the same period—the Pirates were unwilling to give Bream the no-trade clause he demanded.

"I would have signed at their price if I could have had a no-trade," he said at the time. "I was going to take a million dollars less money to sign with the Pirates and I didn't want to look like a fool by being traded to Atlanta a week later."

The Pirates wouldn't cave, and while team president Carl Barger admitted Bream's three knee surgeries in 1989 were a factor, he said of the clause, "We can't get into that. We can't invest millions of dollars in players and be restricted like that."

During his six seasons in Pittsburgh, Bream and Drabek became close. They rode to the ballpark together, and Michele Bream and Kristy Drabek would take their kids—the Bream boys, Michael and Tyler, and the Drabeks' sons, Justin and Kyle—to Chuck E. Cheese's. The Breams were even the godparents of the Drabek children.

No longer teammates, Bream said they "still had a pretty good friendship at that point in time."

The former Cy Young Award winner's first pitch—a breaking ball—sailed into the dirt behind Bream. The second was high and outside, and the third again missed on the outside (despite catcher Mike "Spanky" LaValliere's attempt to frame the pitch, umpire John McSherry didn't bite). Bream's bat never left his shoulder as he took first base on a pitch that LaValliere had to stand up to catch.

"I will not beat myself up trying to figure out what happened," Drabek said later. "I will not sit there all winter and wonder why."

Four pitches and just one close to the strike zone. Maybe it was Drabek's workload—he was on the mound for the third time in the series and the final offering to Bream was his 129th pitch—that led to the blowup. Then again, it could have been that the Braves first baseman had already burned him for a double in the seventh inning. Or it could be something else that had Drabek walking him.

"The way the game works, that mind starts to work a little bit," Bream said. "I don't know if he was thinking about me being at the plate and saying 'I don't want him to do anything against me.' I don't know. I don't know what was going through Doug's mind.

"I just know the things that predicated me coming to the plate were things that could rattle a pitcher a little bit and cause him to thinking, 'What in the world is going on here?' and thus he walked me on four straight pitches. I like to think he knew that I would have ended the ball game right then if he would have pitched to me. I had already hit a double against him that night too. I don't know if that was going through his mind a little bit too. I don't know."

As Drabek told the *New York Times*, facing his friend certainly played a part. "I didn't want to lay one in there to Sid. I wound up overthrowing."

But in truth, Drabek's unraveling could have also had a lot to do with the events that led to Bream coming to bat with the tying run on first base.

The right-hander, who won 15 games with a 2.77 ERA in 34 starts in 1992, had been cruising before the ninth. He gave up five hits, allowed just one runner past second base through eight innings, and at one point retired nine straight.

Drabek stood just three outs from the World Series with Pendleton and Justice starting off the inning. They may have been the reigning MVP (Pendleton) and 1990 Rookie of the Year (Justice), but Pendleton was 0-for-15 vs. Drabek in the series, 0-for-3 on the night, and 6-for-29 in the NLCS, while Justice was hitting .181 (2 for 11) against Drabek and was also hitless in three at-bats.

Pendleton was never aware of those struggles, though, even decades later.

"The funny thing when you're in a situation like that you don't think about what you did against a guy over a course of a year, because to this point I didn't know that I'd struggled against him until you said that right now," he said.

As the Braves ran off the field in the middle of the ninth, the third baseman says there was a peace over him. "I knew we were going to win that game," he recalls.

Leading the series 3–1 after a 6–4 victory at Three Rivers Stadium, the Braves dropped the next two games by a combined 20–5. That included a 13–4 rout in Game Six that saw Tom Glavine last just one inning as he gave up seven earned runs on six hits with zero strikeouts.

If there was tension, it was broken when Cox stopped the players twenty minutes before the game. "Hey," he told them. "Ted wants to talk to you guys."

Owner Ted Turner came bounding in, and the players turned in their chairs. He made eye contact with each of them before saying "Guys, listen. Do me a favor: go out and have fun tonight. Let's just go out and have fun.

"Hell, you guys have made me a lot of money. Each and every one of you guys in this room is going to get raises."

And with that he walked out of the room.

The Braves were no strangers to rallies, piling up 39 come-from-behind wins—including nine walk-off victories—with only the Cardinals (46) and Pirates (40) totaling more among NL teams. A 2–0 deficit wasn't anything they hadn't overcome before.

"Literally our team believed that we could come back no matter what the situation was," Bream said. "Going into that ninth inning, I know there was a lot of optimism on the Braves' part that we could still win this ball game."

Pendleton drove the 1–1 pitch into the right field corner, just inside the line and out of reach of Pittsburgh's Cecil Espy, and the Brave cruised into second, clapping his hands with a standup double.

The ball was clearly fair, but that Ed Montague had to make the call from first base brought further attention to the fact that the umpire crew was down to five members.

Home plate umpire John McSherry began feeling dizzy when the Pirates batted in the top of the first. When the Braves came up an inning later, McSherry walked down the first-base line and put his hands on his knees. Bill White, the president of the NL, saw it and called McSherry over. He was pulled from his position and was replaced by Randy Marsh, forcing Montague to move from right field to first base.

"There I was, seven innings away from finishing the season, and I wind up in the hospital," McSherry told the *Chicago Tribune.* "It was very embarrassing."

It wasn't the first or last time McSherry would leave a game under similar circumstances. He battled weight problems for much of his career—McSherry had a listed weight of 328 pounds—and exited five games in five years due to heat exhaustion, dehydration, or dizziness.

On April 1, 1996, in Cincinnati, he held his hand up to signal the rest of his crew for assistance just seven pitches into the game. Moments later, as McSherry began walking to the tunnel leading to the umpire's locker room, he collapsed. The Reds' trainer began administering CPR and was joined by Expos' staff and doctors who had been watching in the stands. He was taken to the University of Cincinnati Hospital, where he was pronounced dead due to a massive heart attack. He was fifty-one.

After Pendleton's double, the specter of hope filled the crowd, and the war chant and tomahawk chop followed as the left-handed Justice stepped in. His looping swing connected on a ball on the outside half of the plate, sending a routine grounder to second baseman José Lind.

Lind was in the midst of his finest defensive season in six years in Pittsburgh, committing just six errors in 1,190⅔ innings with a .992 fielding percentage, and had been awarded his only Gold Glove earlier in the day.

But this moment would define a season, and a career, as Lind went to his right and missed the ball, which careened off his glove and into the outfield as Justice took first and Pendleton advanced to third.

"It could turn out to be the biggest error of his life," CBS announcer Tim McCarver said.

Cameras cut to the crowd, where Turner and smiling former president and Georgia native Jimmy Carter high-fived.

"What can you say?" Pirates manager Jim Leyland later told reporters. "He's a Gold Glove fielder and he makes that play ten times out of ten. But it happens. That's baseball. I have no problems with José. . . . We got here together. We win together and we lose together."

Said Braves second baseman Mark Lemke, "You're talking about a guy who never makes an error, a Gold Glove second baseman and I, just looking at him as my counterpart on the other club, was just amazed at his defensive ability. He made an error and I said 'You know, that might open the door for us.'"

Still, Drabek had worked his way out of trouble three innings earlier after Atlanta loaded the bases with no outs on three straight base hits. Then Jeff Blauser hit a line drive to third baseman Jeff King, who doubled-up Lemke, who was between third and home. Pendleton then flied out to end the threat.

"My heart just jumped out of my chest when we had the bases loaded, hit two line drives, and wound up without any runs," Cox said.

But after Drabek walked Bream, loading the bases with that array of off-the-mark pitches, Leyland had seen enough, ending Drabek's night in favor of closer Stan Belinda.

"Drabek is a big-game pitcher, and I felt good with him for the first two batters of the inning," said Leyland. "But you could tell when he faced Sid he was trying too hard, and didn't have it at that point."

Belinda would first have to contend with Ron Gant, who was hitting .190 (4-for-21) in the series—but two of those four hits were home runs, including a grand slam off of Bob Walk in Game Two.

"When that inning got going, I thought Ron Gant was going to hit a grand slam. Game over. I really did," Pendleton said.

He came close, driving the second pitch to left field, though it fell at the warning track and into the glove of Barry Bonds.

"Any time Ronnie hits a ball you believe there's a pretty good chance of it going out of the ballpark," Bream said. "He just got underneath it just a little bit too much."

But Gant had succeeded in cutting the Pittsburgh lead in half as Pendleton came home with the Braves' first run. Though as the third baseman made his way back to the dugout, McCarver addressed the reality of the situation.

"Everyone exploding here in the stadium as though something good happened, but something bad happened for Atlanta," he said. "Something good happened for the Pirates. They got the sacrifice fly to left field and not to center or right, because the tying run is the guy who is on second base and that's David Justice."

Belinda did his part to change that, walking catcher Damon Berryhill on a 3–1 fastball that looked to be a strike, but Marsh gave Berryhill the base and LaValliere was left barking at the umpire.

"I thought we could get a double-play ground ball with Berryhill, but we walked him, unfortunately," said Leyland.

With the bases loaded again, Cox opted to pinch-hit Brian Hunter for Rafael Belliard, who popped out to Lind in the grass behind second base to leave the Braves down to their last out. Needing Francisco Cabrera to bat in the pitcher's spot, Atlanta had no regulars on their bench to pinch-run for Bream, though to this day he contests that Cox did have options.

"He had every pitcher that could have run for me," Bream said. "As I say, they could have been into the dugout and into the clubhouse before I got home."

The Braves had a bigger problem on their hands if they couldn't break through in the ninth, as Cox had used

Belliard to hit for starting second baseman Lemke, and then removed him with Hunter.

"He had nobody to play second base, so that would have been his big dilemma," Bream said.

Years before, Bream was still a threat on the basepaths, having stolen 13 bases in 1986 when he was with the Pirates.

"In Pittsburgh I stole bases quite frequently; not a Rickey Henderson or an Otis Nixon or anything like that, but 13 stolen bases for a first baseman in a season isn't a bad tally," he said.

The 6-foot-4 215-pounder wasn't necessarily fast, but he was adept at reading pitchers and picking his spots.

"I was an individual that loved to be aggressive," he said. "Even though I was big, I loved to be aggressive on the basepaths. I would go first to third with the best of them on my team because I knew how to run the bases, I knew how to get that quick first step."

He still knew how to be opportunistic, swiping six bases in '92, and he was never caught once, but time and the operating table had robbed Bream of wanting to play the way he used to. "When I had my knee surgeries it totally took me out of the way I loved to play the game," Bream said.

He used his old tricks of the basepaths to his advantage as he stood on second with Cabrera at bat, Bream a relative non-factor despite representing the go-ahead run. He took a big lead, a risk that could have been his legacy if Belinda would have shown any interest.

"In retrospect, in hindsight, if they would have done something there would have been the good chance I could have been the goat in a hurry," Bream said. "But thankfully they didn't. That's what I was counting on. That's why I got an extra step or two."

Added to the Braves' roster on August 31, Cabrera had all of 11 at-bats, including a lineout in the ninth inning of Game Six in his previous plate appearance of the postseason. But the Dominican catcher had two home runs in that small sample size and the previous season hit one down the left-field line off Belinda in Atlanta.

History nearly repeated itself as the right-hander, who was ahead in the count 2–0, sent Belinda's next pitch—a fastball—toward deep left field. But it hooked foul. Tracking the flight of the ball, Cabrera kicked his leg out as he watched it sail left into the stands.

Marsh was known as a hitter-friendly umpire, and with Belinda missing on pitches he believed were strikes, Belinda had to adjust. "They were called balls. I had to throw strikes," he said. "Every pitch was big, but this is what I get paid to do."

Belinda followed with another fastball—this time high and outside—and Cabrera poked it through shortstop and third base toward Bonds.

"I said, 'Well, I got a green light and I've got to hit the ball good.' I knew I had to be ready," Cabrera said. "The guy's tough, but there was no tomorrow."

When Cabrera had come to bat, center fielder Andy Van Slyke—who had just claimed his fifth consecutive Gold Glove—had suggested Bonds take a few steps in. The eventual MVP responded with his middle finger.

"He turned and looked at me and gave me the international peace sign," Van Slyke told MLB Network in 2011. "So I said, 'Fine, you play where you want.'"

In his defense, Bonds was no slouch either, claiming the third of five consecutive Gold Gloves in 1992, and he won eight over his career. But he was too far back to field Cabrera's hit and had to race toward his left.

Justice scored, and as Bream chugged toward third he kept going. If he was given the stop sign, Bream didn't realize it. "To this day, I have no idea what [third base coach] Jimy Williams did," Bream said. "If he did, I certainly didn't see it."

From the dugout, Pendleton and the rest of the Braves were screaming, "Go Sid! Go Sid! Go Sid!" Pendleton recalls. "That's the only thing that's on our mind 'Go Sid! Go Sid!'"

As Bream closed in on the plate, LaValliere had to move to his right toward first base to field Bonds's throw— a one-hopper that landed down the line—and as the catcher reached back, Bream's left foot reached the plate seemingly at the same time.

"SAFE!" Marsh called in a play that's still debated years later in Atlanta and Pittsburgh.

"Sid was a good baserunner," said Pendleton. "His knees took the speed out of him, but one thing I did know about Sid, he was going to run those bases properly. I knew that for a fact and the only thing saved us and saved Sid that night was [that] Sid run the bases exactly the way the bases should have been run."

In the Braves' radio booth, the legendary Skip Caray gave arguably his most iconic call:

"Two balls, one strike. What tension! A lot of room in right center. If he hits one there, we can dance in the streets. The 2–1: Swung, line drive left field! One run is in. Here comes Bream; here's the throw to the plate. He is . . . safe!

"BRAVES WIN, BRAVES WIN, BRAVES WIN, BRAVES WIN, BRAVES WIN!!!

"They may have to hospitalize Sid Bream. He's down at the bottom of a huge pile at the plate. They help him to his feet. Frank Cabrera got the game-winner. The Atlanta Braves are National League champions again; this crowd is going berserk!"

From his bed at Piedmont Hospital, McSherry, the man who would have been the one to decide that critical play, sided with Marsh.

"Good call," McSherry said. "Randy was in perfect position. He got it right."

Recalls Bream, "I knew that I had to get down and a lot of people had said over the years, 'Man, you made a great hook slide.' It was no hook slide about that.

"I went straight into the base and thankfully Barry Bonds's one-hop throw to Spanky was just a little bit up that line that he had to reach and come back to try and put that tag on, and I was able to get my foot in there before he touched my bottom foot."

Bream was mobbed, as Justice grabbed him around the neck and rolled underneath him, and he was piled on by a parade of Berryhill, Blauser, Hunter, reliever David Nied, outfielder Otis Nixon, and on and on. Turner ran out on the field, followed by Jimmy Carter. Overcome by the moment, the former president grabbed Williams and kissed him.

"It was the most exciting athletic event that I've ever seen," Carter said. "I was more thrilled and excited with Sid Bream's slide than any other thing I've ever seen in any kind of sport. I remember it all very well."

And like everyone else watching it unfold, Carter couldn't believe Bream kept running past third or that he beat Bonds's throw.

"We didn't know if he was going to make it or not," Carter said. "We didn't have any idea he was going to run from third into home. It was really amazing to all of us."

Back in the World Series for the second straight year, the Braves again fell short, this time losing to the Blue Jays in six games. But they would be back.

Van Slyke sat on the grass watching Atlanta celebrate, a third straight NLCS loss that would mark the beginning of the end for the Pirates.

"All the stars lined up against us," the center fielder told the *Pittsburgh Post-Gazette* about Game Seven.

Bonds and Drabek left for San Francisco and Houston respectively, after the season. Van Slyke stayed until after the 1994 season. And after 1994, Pittsburgh would fail to make the playoffs for twenty seasons.

Bream did his part to help the Pirates, having worked as a hitting coach for one of their Class-A affiliates, the State College Spikes, in 2008. "I can't stand to lose and we've been doing an awful lot of that," he told MLB.com at the time.

In June 2012, the Braves celebrated the twentieth anniversary of The Slide with a bobblehead—both Bream and LaValliere gave their permission—and Bream feigned replicating the moment as he jogged down the third base line and stuck his leg out before wagging his finger toward the crowd.

The Braves were playing their 1992 Series opponent, the Blue Jays, that day, and there was a connection to the Pirates. Doug Drabek's son, Kyle, was one of Toronto's pitchers, starting a game on the day before the festivities.

"It was a weird feeling to have those two teams here and Kyle Drabek on the mound last night," Bream said at the time.

Bream's place in the game boils down to one moment, one that's considered one of the greatest in postseason history. But he's quick to point out that he's not the one truly responsible for it.

"[Cabrera's] the one that deserves all the credit for it all," he said. "Frankie, as everybody says, somebody that was a nobody. 'Who's Frankie Cabrera?' But to come up in a situation like that and to hit the ball that he did, I mean a high outside fastball from a side-armer, and then rip a ball through third base and short without hitting a ground ball . . . I mean, he ripped it.

"He's the one that deserves all the credit for everything. I'm just thankful that I was slow enough that I made it exciting."

Chapter Six

With the Number-One Pick . . .

It was prom night for Jacksonville's Bolles School and the senior was dining at Olive Garden.

That scenario could apply to millions of high school students across the country. Except he was with his parents and Braves scouts, while his girlfriend and buddies were at a beach house preparing for the dance.

Atlanta scout Tony DeMacio told Chipper Jones he could eat anywhere he wanted and the switch-hitting Florida shortstop had opted for the home of endless bread sticks.

"Chipper's big deal was the Olive Garden at that time," his father, Larry Jones Sr., said, laughing.

The Braves had the number-one pick in the 1990 draft and DeMacio, along with cross-checker Dean Jongewaard, had come to check on the signability of Larry Jr., who was better known as Chipper. But Jones's parents couldn't find him.

He finally got hold of Bolles's baseball coach, Don Suriano, with an urgent message.

"They said, 'Get your butt back here now!'" Chipper Jones told ESPN.com in 2010.

He was two hours away and drove down I-95 to Daytona Beach to meet for dinner.

There was no prom night tux, though he was wearing a cast on his right hand, the result of a cracked bone suffered in a fight on the field the day before the state championship game. "The other guys on the club started picking on [another teammate] and he got mad at everybody," Jones said in a 1990 interview with the *Chicago Tribune*. "I just walked in on it. He started yelling at me. I told him to get out of my face. He began pushing me and I hit him."

After dinner they headed to the family's Pierson, Florida, home, and the Joneses made their demand. Larry Sr., who was acting as his son's agent, asked for $300,000. The previous year, top pick Ben McDonald received $275,000 from the Orioles and "I thought that Chipper ought to get basically what Ben McDonald got, plus a little more for inflation," Larry Sr. said.

The Braves, who the year before had given number-two overall pick Tyler Houston a $241,500 signing bonus—a franchise record—countered with $250,000. Father looked at son and said, "Let's go upstairs and talk about it."

"You know, Chipper," Larry Sr. said when they were alone, "we can get a little more than what they're talking about."

"Dad," Chipper recalled to the *St. Louis Post-Dispatch* in 1996, "I just want to go play. I'm going to make my money in the big leagues, not off the deal right here."

The Joneses came back downstairs and came to an agreement on a signing bonus equal to McDonald's as part of a package that included $68,000 to cover Chipper's college education whenever he decided to enroll and a life insurance annuity that increased the total value to $400,000.

"We were in the ballpark right away," Chipper told the Associated Press after the draft. "We said what we wanted and they said what they wanted to give and I said 'Why don't we split the difference both ways.'"

He was signed and sealed and would become the last player DeMacio ever inked before leaving to join the Indians in 1990. The first was Hall of Famer and two-time Cy Young winner Tom Glavine in 1984.

Two weeks after being picked, Jones was in uniform, playing shortstop for the Gulf Coast League's Bradenton Braves. He had an inglorious pro debut, hitting .229/.321/.271 in 140 at-bats, but it was one of the few bumps in a nineteen-year career that is destined to end in Cooperstown.

Jones became an eight-time All-Star, the 1999 National League Most Valuable Player, and a two-time Silver Slugger Award winner. Playing third base for the majority of his career, he amassed 53.2 Wins Above Replacement, per Baseball Reference. Only Hall of Famers Mike Schmidt (73.3), Eddie Mathews (58.6), and Wade Boggs (57.0) were better, and Jones is ahead of George Brett (50.4), Brooks Robinson (39.6), Home Run Baker (37.0), and Ron Santo (36.7), all of whom have already been enshrined.

He hit the third-most home runs of any switch-hitter with 468, behind Mickey Mantle (536) and Eddie Murray (504), and had the second-best average at .303, trailing only Frankie Frisch's .316.

"He was born to play the game," former Atlanta pitcher Tim Hudson said in 2013. "He was born to hit. His career showed it."

Said team president John Schuerholz, "He's a winner. He's a champion, and few players have ever made such a profound impact on one franchise."

Chipper Jones would spend his entire nineteen-year career with the Braves, becoming an eight-time All-Star and the 1999 NL MVP. (*Keith Allison*)

That it was all in a Braves uniform was one of the most remarkable aspects of Jones's career. But that piece of Chipper's path to greatness came down to one simple fact that ultimately worked in a player and franchise's favor: the 1990 draft's top-ranked prospect wasn't interested.

*   *   *   *

"**W**e all heard that Todd Van Poppel didn't want to play here," said Glavine. "I think we all took it personally. I think we were all like 'Okay, screw you. We don't want you to play here.'"

The thought process was that the Braves knew they had a nucleus of good, young players. They had Glavine, along with John Smoltz, Steve Avery, Pete Smith, Mark Lemke, Jeff Blauser, Ron Gant, and David Justice.

"You're looking around going 'We've got some pretty good young players here. I think eventually, we're going to have some success,'" Glavine said. "So we kind of took offense to it."

To be clear, Van Poppel didn't say he wouldn't sign with the Braves. He didn't want to sign with anyone.

"I really have no doubt that if Todd Van Poppel would have shown any interest at all, he probably would have been taken by the Braves," Jones Sr. said.

The 6-foot-5, 205-pound Arlington right-hander was, as Chipper Jones said in '97, "The prize. Everybody else was second." He had a 96-mph fastball and a big, breaking curveball and went 11–4 as a senior with a 1.04 ERA, striking out 169 batters with 38 walks in 101 innings.

But he had already committed to stay in state and pitch for the University of Texas, regardless of where he went in the draft.

Van Poppel had designs on continuing a trajectory that involved college and preserving his amateur status to reach his baseball goals.

"I played in the Mickey Mantle World Series, the Connie Mack World Series. I wanted to go play in the Olympics. I wanted to go play in the College World Series and someday the World Series," Van Poppel told *Creative Loafing* in 2012. "I wanted to go to college and do the college thing. I was going to school."

Chipper Jones and Van Poppel were not just aware of each other and the talk of either of them going first in the draft. They knew each other. When Jones made his official visit to the University of Miami, Van Poppel was there too, considering whether he would commit to the Hurricanes, which Jones did.

But while Jones wasn't a lock to go to college, the Van Poppels had reiterated the pitcher's stance to the Braves when Bobby Cox—then Atlanta's general manager—had arrived in Dallas to meet with the family. The next day Todd pitched a one-hitter to advance to the Texas state high school semifinals.

The family and Cox didn't discuss contract figures in their meeting. "It was brought up in general terms," Hank Van Poppel, Todd's dad, told the *Atlanta Journal-Constitution*, "but to us it's not a matter of money."

Braves director of scouting Paul Snyder kept calling to see if Van Poppel had changed his mind. So too did Red Murff, who had a unique perspective on the righty considering that people were comparing Todd to Nolan Ryan. Murff, then with the Mets, scouted and signed Ryan in 1965 and only strengthened the nods to "The Ryan Express" by saying Van Poppel had the best arsenal he'd seen since Ryan.

"He has the classic pitcher's body. Tall, rangy, loose arm, wide shoulders," Murff told the Associated Press. "I couldn't pass this kid if I had the first pick."

But the day before the draft, Cox had called the Van Poppels to tell them the Braves had decided they were passing on Todd.

"He wished us good luck and said he'd be watching the next two or three years," Hank Van Poppel told the *Journal-Constitution*. "It's something we've said all along. I've tried to keep his options open, but Todd is set on attending the University of Texas."

The belief was, that with Van Poppel out of the equation, the Braves would pick between Jones—who hit .488 as a senior with five home runs, 10 doubles, and 25 RBIs, and also stole 14 bases, along with a 7–3 record on the mound and a 1.00 ERA—and power-hitting first baseman Mark Newfield of Huntington Beach, California, who was being projected as an outfielder.

In truth they had already decided on Jones, whom Cox had traveled to Jacksonville to see play four times, and it was one of those last visits that Larry Jones Sr. believes sealed the deal for his son.

It was the finals of the district tournament and Cox was joined by a contingent that included Snyder, minor-league field coordinator Bobby Dews, and assistant director of scouting Rod Gilbreath. Jones came up to bat in the first inning and hit a home run right-handed, then later hit another left-handed on the first swing, the ball landing in the street behind the park.

Larry Jones looked over at his wife, Lynne, and said, "That may have just made him the first pick in the draft."

Moments later, Snyder came by, looking at the couple as he said, "Nice touch."

There remains some question as to who was all on board with Jones going number one. In 2008, Hank Aaron told the *Journal-Constitution* about an exchange with Cox in which Aaron, then the organization's farm director, told the GM, "Y'all better go and get Chipper Jones."

Aaron had already talked to Hank Van Poppel and knew there was no way he was signing, but Cox sought pitching and the Texas right-hander was his choice.

"That's who Bobby wanted," Aaron told the *Journal-Constitution*. "But every time you listen, it's always like, 'Oh, yeah. We always wanted to sign Chipper Jones.' The only reason they didn't take Van Poppel was because of what I told them about what his daddy told me."

Regardless of who was leading the push, it was that signability meeting that finally put it all into focus for the Joneses.

"That was the first time we really felt confident that he was going to go with the first pick," Jones Sr. said.

They had been expecting Chipper to go to the Mariners, who held the number-six selection, should he fall that far, though the father had hopes that his son would wind up with the Dodgers. They picked ninth and it was unlikely that Chipper would last that long, but that was Larry Jones Sr.'s team.

The call came at 1:22 p.m. on June 4, 1990, and Chipper Jones could finally allow himself to believe what seemed a lock after that meeting with Braves scouts.

"It baffles the mind," Jones said to the *Orlando Sentinel*. "Being number one baffles my mind. I knew it could happen, but I've tried all morning not to get too keyed up, just in case there was a letdown."

Tony Clark followed Jones by going to the Tigers, with Mike Lieberthal (Phillies) third, Alex Fernandez (White Sox) fourth, Kurt Miller (Pirates) fifth, Marc Newfield (Mariners) sixth, Dan Wilson (Reds) seventh, Tim Costo (Indians) eighth, Ronnie Walden (Dodgers) ninth, and Carl Everett (Yankees) rounding out the top ten.

While the picks came, Van Poppel was fishing, and while his disinterest in this draft or being taken in it kept the first thirteen teams away, it didn't work on the Athletics.

The defending World Series champions gambled they could be the ones to sway him to put off college, what with those rings, and the fact that Oakland had produced three straight American League Rookies of the Year in Jose Canseco in 1986, Mark McGwire in 1987, and Walt Weiss in 1988.

"I think he should sign," McGwire told the *Dallas Times Herald* at the time. "With the rumor of the money they're talking, I don't see how he says no. He can go to college three or four times over with that kind of money."

Van Poppel agreed to a $1.2 million contract that included a $600,000 signing bonus, or a package that was nearly $1 million more than Jones got with the top pick. Van Poppel's deal was the largest ever for a draft pick.

"After knowing a few things about the major leagues since [being drafted], I've realized everybody should leave their options open," Van Poppel said at his introductory press conference with the A's.

"When they first came and talked to me, they didn't say anything about not going to Texas. That impressed me. This is a classy organization."

Said Hank Van Poppel, who had spent weeks dissuading his son's suitors, "There's no question I'm surprised to be here today. Todd knew he could probably sign for more money three years from now if he stayed healthy. He knew he could have a good career in baseball and still go to school. But he also knew the chances of being drafted by the Oakland A's three years from now were slim and none."

It's worth noting that the Braves did present a similar package to Van Poppel. "It was in the same ballpark and we could have compromised," Gilbreath said to the *Philadelphia Inquirer*. "But we never got positive feedback from him or his father."

Of course, the Braves were in the middle of a seventh straight losing season; they would go 65–97 in 1990. The A's presented a combination of winning and an ability to foster and develop talent that won out—even if, after being picked, Todd Van Poppel's first reaction was, "This is so stupid. We made our position clear, didn't we?"

In an interview with the *Chicago Tribune*, Deron Gustafson, a Texas assistant and son of head coach Cliff Gustafson, provided a quote that would prove ominous for Van Poppel.

"It's great for the kid," he said, "but how can you give a million dollars to an eighteen-year-old who hasn't proven himself?"

The hype didn't die down as Van Poppel appeared on the first issue of baseball card pricing guide Beckett's "Future Stars" . . . alongside Ryan.

With Van Poppel signed to a major-league contract, the A's forced his progress, and despite 6.1 walks per nine innings and a 3.47 ERA at Double-A Huntsville, he made his debut with Oakland in September 1991.

He floundered, allowing five earned runs on seven hits in 4⅔ innings, and didn't return to the majors until 1993. In 104 games with the A's, Van Poppel had a 5.75 ERA before bouncing around with the Tigers, Rangers, Pirates, Cubs, and Reds. He attempted to make the Mets in 2005, but unceremoniously left camp on March 8 and retired.

It was all punctuated by his 1996 season, in which he had a 9.06 ERA that ranks as the highest in history with at least 90 innings.

Van Poppel was the most glaring example, but he was far from the only first-round mistake the A's made that year. They took four pitchers in all—Don Peters from St. Francis College in New York at number twenty-six, UCLA star Dave Zancanaro thirty-fourth, and Texas All-American Kirk Dressendorfer thirty-sixth—a collection of arms that baseball card manufacturer Classic Games, Inc., further hyped with a 1991 card fearing the quartet holding oversize ace playing cards with "Future Aces" underneath.

"Oakland had four of the first thirty-six picks of the 1990 draft," the back of the card read. "The A's chose flame throwing pitchers with each of these valued picks. The A's are banking on Todd Van Poppel, Don Peters, David Zancanaro, and Kirk Dressendorfer to carry the team into the 21st century."

Bad luck certainly played its part in the disaster that draft would become as all but Van Poppel had some variation of arm surgery—Zancanaro had a torn rotator cuff, Dressendorfer suffered a tear in his shoulder, and Peters underwent a shoulder procedure similar to Tommy John—and Van Poppel was said to limit his range of motion with excessive weightlifting.

"It's very frustrating," A's assistant GM Walt Jock-etty told a McClatchy News Service writer in 1993. "We were expecting one or two of them to be here by now. It's slowed down, but we certainly haven't given up."

None of them would make it past the mid-1990s as A's, let alone the twenty-first century as expected, as Peters and Zancanaro never reached the majors and Dressendorfer's career included seven games with a 5.45 ERA in 1991.

While Van Poppel was being rushed through the minors with that record contract in hand, the Braves were playing it safe with Jones.

After spending the 1991 season—his first full year in pro ball—at Class-A Macon where he hit .326/.407/.518 with 24 doubles, 11 triples, and 15 home runs in 473 at-bats with 40 stolen bases, Jones was to start 1992 in Double-A Greenville, bypassing high-A Durham altogether.

Larry Sr. and Lynne had planned to go to watch the Braves' major-league spring training in West Palm Beach, Florida, and they stopped by Dodgertown in Vero Beach where the Greenville Braves were playing. After the game, the Joneses checked into their hotel and Chipper came over. Larry Sr. could tell something was wrong.

"I just got demoted to Durham," a dejected Chipper told him.

They all went out to eat. Chuck LaMar, the Braves' director of player development and scouting, walked in and came past the Joneses table.

"Oh, I bet I'm the hot topic of conversation tonight," he said.

The next day, Chipper was playing with Durham. While Larry Sr. was watching, LaMar approached him.

"Let me explain to you why we demoted him," LaMar said.

"Chuck, you don't have to tell me this," Jones responded. "This is ya'll's decision."

"Nah, I want you to know what we wanted for Chipper is to get off to a good start and promote him, as opposed to getting off to a bad start in Greenville and us having to demote him [during the season]."

After 70 games with the Durham Bulls, Jones was back with Greenville, where he hit nine homers with a .346 average and 42 RBIs in 67 games.

"[He] just took off and I go back to that conversation I had and that thought process the Braves had at the time of promoting as opposed to demoting," Larry Sr. said.

Mark Lemke had met Jones in 1990 when he was at rookie ball in Bradenton on a rehab assignment and told a newly-signed Chipper, "I'll see you in a few years up here in Atlanta."

After a September call-up in 1993, it seemed that Lemke would see him sooner rather than later, as the Braves wanted Jones to break into the majors in '94 and contend for their opening in left field. They had cut Ron Gant, who broke his leg in a dirt-bike accident, one week after he had inked a one-year, $5.5 million deal.

"He looked like a different guy to me," Lemke said of Jones. "He had just gotten out of high school back then, but boy, when he developed and grew into a man, it was incredible to watch."

His transition to left field was an easy one, and Jones was making noise with his bat, hitting .371 with two homers and eight RBIs.

But on March 19, four innings after hitting a home run against the Yankees in Ft. Lauderdale, Jones hit a ground ball to shortstop. New York first baseman Jim Leyritz had to come off the bag to field the throw, and Jones, trying to avoid the tag, landed awkwardly on his left leg. He crumbled to the ground with a torn anterior cruciate ligament in his left knee.

His season was over.

"That was the toughest thing I've ever had [to deal with]," Jones told the AP in 1996. "It taught me never to take the game for granted, because sometimes I did."

Jones returned in '95, and while the Braves signed Ryan Klesko to play left, they didn't return former MVP third baseman Terry Pendleton. Jones flourished, finishing second in the NL Rookie of the Year race to the Dodgers' Hideo Nomo, as he hit .265/.353/.450 with 22 doubles, three triples, and 23 homers.

The player that at the time of the 1990 draft seemed like a fallback plan would become a fixture and the face of the franchise for nearly two decades.

"From Day One, look, for me, it's the most talented player I've ever played with," Lemke said.

When Jones finally retired in 2012, it was with a final tour that included a litany of gifts along the way. It started with a Stetson hat from the Astros presented by Craig Biggio, and would include a Braves flag from Wrigley Field, third-base bags from the Reds and Yankees, a surfboard via the Padres, a pack of fishing equipment gifted by the Marlins, and a grill and a year's supply of sausages from the Brewers.

From the Braves, Jones would receive a number of gifts: a pool table from his teammates; a plaque made from Turner Field bricks shaped like home plate; and a Hawaiian vacation. They also dedicated an entire weekend to number 10's career.

In his final regular-season home game, a 6–2 victory over the Mets—a team he terrorized throughout his career, hitting .309 with 49 homers and 159 RBIs against them—Jones went 1-for-2 with two walks and a run.

When it was finally over, he climbed into the stands to hug his parents.

"I've been kind of cowboy-ing up all week trying to hold back the tears," Jones said of the buildup. "Obviously, when it comes full circle and you stand there in front of 50,000 people and you tell your mom and dad that you love them, it means a lot to me."

Throughout their son's run, Larry Sr. and Lynne would often make trips to see him play, a front-row seat to a Hall of Fame career.

"With the way things fell at least once or twice a year we'd go up for a long weekend and get to watch him play," Jones Sr. said. "If he would have gone to Seattle, we may never have gotten to see him play."

Where Chipper Jones landed, and that he would walk away at age 40, as the last link to Atlanta's unprecedented run of 14 consecutive division titles, created a charmed baseball life that may not have come so easily if he'd have been picked by another team.

"It was just one of those things where everything kind of fell into the right place at the right time," Larry Sr. said.

*   *   *   *

Chipper Jones looked out into the Turner Field crowd on June 28, 2013, and the sly smile that was a fixture on his weathered face appeared.

"I want to thank Todd Van Poppel tonight," he joked in typical Chipper fashion, the words spilling out of the side of his mouth.

Minutes later, Jones's number 10 was retired by the Braves, with his name and number appearing in a three-dimensional red, white, and blue monument along the facade of the stadium. He joins Hank Aaron, Mathews,

Jones's manager Bobby Cox, and former teammates Tom Glavine, Greg Maddux, and John Smoltz.

Fittingly, Jones's number sits on the third-base side of the park, just above the position he manned.

"It still doesn't seem real," Jones said at the time. "I play baseball. It's not like I cure cancer or anything. It's almost embarrassing to be getting all this attention, all the accolades and whatnot. It's so humbling."

Jones's longtime walk-up music, Ozzy Osbourne's "Crazy Train," blared throughout the stadium as Jones was driven around in the back of a white Camaro.

"The hair on the back of your neck stands up," he said after that ride. "You get chill bumps."

Looking back, Glavine can't help but smile at the debate that raged in 1990. Van Poppel may have been the most sought-after prospect, but in picking Jones, the Braves landed a player that would become an icon.

"It's funny how things work out," Glavine said. "Who knows where this organization ultimately would have been had they drafted Todd Van Poppel and not Chipper Jones."

Chapter Seven

The Three-Headed Monster

Leo Mazzone would take his place in the dugout for his pregame ritual as he watched the opposition take batting practice, making mental note of their swings, their approaches, and where they were putting the ball. It was all invaluable information for the Braves pitching coach.

"I did that every day of my entire career," he said.

With Atlanta in Wrigley Field to play the Cubs, Mazzone walked out and sat on the bench in the visiting dugout when he saw Chicago players Shawon Dunston and Mark Grace behind the batting cage.

"Hey, Leo, you've got a big grin on your face today," Grace called out. "What you smiling about Leo? Oh, let me guess who's pitching today? Glavine. Okay. Who's pitching tomorrow? Smoltz. Who's pitching the third game? Maddux.

"No wonder you've got a smile on your face."

Mazzone laughs, long and loud. "I knew right then and there that we were already in their heads," he said.

The 1990s Braves were, more than anything, all about pitching. They won National League MVPs with Terry Pendleton in 1991 and Chipper Jones in 1999, but the foundation of Atlanta's reign were the Hall of Fame arms.

Tom Glavine. Greg Maddux. John Smoltz.

"I called them 'The Trifecta,' because that's exactly what they are," said HOFer Wade Boggs.

From 1991 to 1998, they claimed six Cy Young Awards, with one of those coming from Maddux in 1992 before he went to Atlanta and claimed the next three. In that eight-year span only the Expos' Pedro Martinez in 1997 could pry the award away from a player that wasn't, or wouldn't eventually, be in a Braves uniform.

During their ten seasons together, the Big Three combined to win nine division titles, three pennants, and the 1995 World Series.

"I think we felt like if we went into the series and the three of us were pitching, worst case scenario, it was going to be two out of three," Glavine said. "Hopefully we would sweep."

From the time Maddux arrived in 1993 via free agency until Smoltz underwent Tommy John surgery—costing him the 2000 season—the trio were a combined 342–160, winning two-thirds of their decisions.

With a .673 winning percentage during that stretch, Glavine, Maddux, and Smoltz were 48 points higher than the MLB-best Braves as a whole (.625) and 76 better than the Yankees' .597.

"If you have great pitching like that, you've got a great chance to win a lot of ball games," said former Braves manager Bobby Cox. "We felt good about it."

There were two vantage points of Glavine, Maddux, and Smoltz's dominance: You loved it or you dreaded it, and it had everything to do with what uniform you were wearing.

Said second baseman Mark Lemke, who spent five seasons with the trio, "Back in those days there were teams looking to go anywhere on the road but come to Atlanta. There was a lot of fear in the opponents' eyes. They knew they had their work cut out for them when they came to Atlanta."

Brian Jordan was among those who saw it from both sides. He had played against them during six seasons with the Cardinals, then joined Atlanta as a free agent in '99, and a big reason was to have the Big Three on his side.

"Those pitchers were challenges and I loved it, but it wasn't good for the team, because we would, you know, most likely lose more than win," he said. "I knew I had a chance to win every day with those guys on the mound, so for me it was all about winning a World Series and having that great opportunity because of those guys."

Only two rotations ever can match the Braves' three Hall of Famers: the Dodgers' Don Drysdale, Sandy Koufax, and Don Sutton and the Indians' Bob Feller, Bob Lemon, and Early Wynn. The Los Angeles entry played just one year together (1966), and while Cleveland's legends were together for eight seasons, their winning percentage of .628 is 45 points behind Glavine, Maddux, and Smoltz's time together in the rotation.

Simply put: No rotation in the game's history can match what the Braves had during their run together.

"We never dreamt that we might be apart," Smoltz said. "So we played as if we were going to be together forever."

Forming that history-making threesome was the result of two trades: one that happened, and another that ultimately fell apart.

*   *   *   *

Tom Glavine walked into a Toledo hotel room on August 12, 1987, having allowed one run over seven innings for Triple-A Richmond in a loss to the Mud Hens when his phone rang. It was his manager, Roy Majtyka.

"The Braves just traded Doyle Alexander," Majtyka told him, "and they're calling you up to the big leagues."

"I'm what?" Glavine replied.

Four nights later he would make his major-league debut in the Astrodome. He was more consumed with trying to find enough tickets for the family and friends that would want to be there than worrying about who the Braves got in return.

That deal became the springboard for the Braves dynasty.

Alexander, 36, would go 9–0 in helping the Tigers claim the American League East, but in return for the veteran, Atlanta received a 19-year-old with a big arm and control issues who had 86 strikeouts and 81 walks in 130 Double-A innings.

John Smoltz.

"We want to keep adding arms and build for the future," then-general manager Bobby Cox told the *Atlanta Journal–Constitution*. "That doesn't mean we don't want to win now. Trading Doyle doesn't affect that.

"Our plan has been to get as many good arms as we can. There's no question Doyle is one of the top pitchers in the game. But right now, he's better off with a team that's a contender."

The Braves were far from that, on their way to 92 losses in 1987, which was their fourth straight losing season. Alexander was available and Detroit was biting, but all that remained open was what Atlanta would get in return.

Scout John Hagemann had seen Smoltz all of 2⅔ innings and lobbied hard to Cox to ask for him in return. But they also liked Steve Searcy, a left-hander who had a 4.22 ERA in 10 starts for the Mud Hens that season, but had better control.

So the Braves left it up to the Tigers to make the final call.

Detroit GM Bill Lajoie wasn't allowed to make maneuvers on his own—the result of a conflict with team president Jim Campbell—and while he wanted to send Searcy to the Braves, he was overruled.

"When I asked various people, the consensus was [to keep] Searcy," Lajoie said in a 2009 radio interview. "The consensus was that he was closer [to the majors]. I didn't feel like I was on real solid ground at the time. I went with the consensus, knowing full well that I should have traded Searcy."

With a 4–10 record and 5.68 ERA in 21 starts for Glens Falls, Smoltz—an East Lansing, Michigan, native who grew up a Tigers fan—initially saw it as the latest setback in a year full of them when he got the call that he had been dealt to Atlanta.

"I didn't know what my future held, and how I was going to get out of this funk, and then the trade happened," Smoltz said, "and I just associated [it with a] bad year—this is bad if somebody doesn't want me."

But he remembers it taking about forty-eight hours for him to change that perspective. The Braves were bad, but that also meant he could see the field in the majors much quicker than he would have had he remained with Detroit and had to battle veterans for playing time.

"The opportunity that I was going to get to pitch at a young age at the professional level was what took me to the next level and pushed me to regain my hope again," Smoltz said.

Since he was dealt for a major leaguer, Smoltz had to move up a level, meaning he would be going to Triple A. But he continued to struggle in Richmond and was sent to the Instructional League. That was when he met Mazzone.

"I was a lost puppy out of Detroit," Smoltz said. "We didn't have any pitching coaches [with the Tigers]. We had rovers and I didn't know what I was doing . . . I was throwing side sessions like a regular game trying to figure it out."

It was just the pitcher, coach, and a catcher on the backfield and Mazzone asked Smoltz simply, "Show me your delivery."

Smoltz's mechanics had been tweaked with the Tigers, and while he continued to throw hard, the adjustment could at least be pointed to as part of his control issues.

"I was kind of beaten up mentally and just thought that I wasn't very good," Smoltz said.

"That's great," Mazzone said as he threw his first pitch.

"What?" Smoltz replied.

"No, that's perfect," Mazzone said. "We just need to upgrade your pitches. If we upgraded your pitches and improve your command, you're going to be fine."

"That," Smoltz says now, "is exactly what happened."

In 1988 he made 20 starts for Richmond, with a 2.79 ERA and 10–5 mark, and less than a year after the trade, Smoltz made his MLB debut. He gave up just one run on four hits over eight innings against the Mets. A season later, he was an All-Star with a 2.94 ERA in 29 starts.

"I knew that if I was going to make this trade lopsided I was going to have an opportunity to pitch at a young age [in the majors], and I'm glad I did," Smoltz said.

Searcy, the player the Braves could have had in Smoltz's place, did reach the majors, but his career would amount to five seasons, a 6–13 record, and 5.68 ERA.

Smoltz or Searcy—all Glavine cared was it gave him his chance.

"I obviously knew who Doyle Alexander was," Glavine said. "Didn't know John; knew we had gotten a good, young pitcher in the trade, but ultimately all I knew was 'Hey, he got traded' and that was ultimately my opportunity to get to the big leagues."

He made nine starts after Alexander was traded, then followed with 34 more in taking a league-high 17 losses in 1988. But three years later he rattled off the first of three straight seasons of 20 or more wins and claimed his first Cy Young.

He was bound for Cooperstown, as was Smoltz, forever tied in that rotation and a deal that was life-altering for each.

"It's funny how those kinds of things work out," Glavine said. "Yeah, it's kind of ironic how those pieces work together."

*   *   *   *

In the winter of 1992, Terry Pendleton was called into the trailer at the Braves' West Palm Beach facility that served as the makeshift office of general manager John Schuerholz. The reigning NL MVP walked in to find Cox there as well.

"What do you think of this?" the GM asked him.

The topic of conversation: Barry Bonds.

The Pirates' left fielder, and two-time MVP, was in the last season of his contract, and Schuerholz wanted to trade for him. But the GM had questions about Bonds's ego—he would, in his Giants days, have four lockers and a leather recliner.

"That was his major concern," Pendleton said, "and I looked him dead in the eye and I said, 'John, let me worry about that.'

"I said, 'You go get him. If we can get him, go get him. I don't know how it's going to play out, but if you can go get him, go get him. I'll handle that. I'll worry about that. I'll take control of that. You don't have to worry about that.'"

Ultimately, Schuerholz believed that the culture Cox had built would win out.

"Bobby looked beyond that when we talked about Barry Bonds," Schuerholz said. "He just looked at him as a great talent.

"We believe and we always believed, he and I both, if there was someone like that who was more in-dividualistic-centric than team-centric, then coming to his environment where this whole place is full of team-centric people and attitude and style, that it would win this person over."

Glavine heard the rumblings. He had moved to Atlanta full-time and was certain the Braves would be adding a once-in-a-generation bat to their lineup.

"I was much more in tune with the rumors and what people were talking about and I, like so many people, was convinced that we were going to get Barry," he said. "That's who we were going after. I know we were. To this day I know we were. I don't know what happened."

Over several days, Schuerholz negotiated with Pirates GM Ted Simmons, coming to an agreement over the phone on a package that would see reliever Alejandro Pena, outfielder Keith Mitchell, and an undecided prospect go to Pittsburgh for Bonds.

Schuerholz informed his players, which created a sticky situation with Pena. The Pirates were adamant about wanting the pitcher, who had just signed as a free agent February 28. That meant the Braves needed his permission to include him in any deal, and Schuerholz had to get Pena to sign a form consenting to the trade.

"He begrudgingly, but willingly finally, at the end, signed," Schuerholz said.

The GM went to bed thinking he had landed Bonds in a deal that, years later, would have looked like robbery. He went to his office the next day making preparations to announce the trade and called Simmons to go over the timing of their organizations' releases of the news.

One problem: The Pirates were backing out.

When manager Jim Leyland was informed of the return for Bonds, he went to team president Carl Barger's office and voiced his disapproval. He had no interest in playing the season without his best player, even if he was in a walk year.

"There was a lot of speculation in the media," Schuerholz said, "but there was much more work being done behind the scenes and undercover that nobody knew about, except Ted Simmons and myself, and eventually their owner and eventually their manager—and eventually, the deal blew up."

Bonds was never aware of what could have been, telling the *New York Times* in 2006, when he was a little more than a year from passing Braves icon Hank Aaron for the all-time home run lead, "I [just] know Leyland stopped them from trading me."

With Glavine, Smoltz, and budding star Steve Avery already in their rotation, the Braves moved forward with a different plan.

"We immediately began to focus on the best free-agent pitcher in the marketplace," Schuerholz said.

During the 1992 All-Star Game in San Diego, the Cubs wanted to meet with Maddux and his agent, Scott Boras. Contract negotiations with the free-agent-to-be stalled the previous December, and if Maddux had any thoughts of them picking back up, they were all but dashed in that July talk with Cubs GM Larry Himes.

"They told me I had never won 20 games or a Cy Young," Maddux told the Arlington Heights *Daily Herald* in 2012. "They basically told me I wasn't very good."

Never mind he'd already won 67 games the previous four years combined. Maddux would reach 20 wins that season and win a Cy Young.

If Himes's harsh words were a challenge—one that Maddux met—he didn't increase the team's bid by much. Offered a five-year deal for $27.5 million in July of 1991, the Cubs came back with a package believed to be between that initial offer and $30.5 million for five years.

Maddux rejected that deal. He marched into free agency, and nearly into pinstripes.

On the morning of December 2, 1992, Maddux called Boras, telling him he wanted to play for the Yankees. The agent proposed a five-year, $37.5 million contract, one that, if agreed upon, Maddux would sign immediately.

Less than two hours later, Schuerholz made his own play with a deal of more than $5 million per season. It piqued Maddux's interest, and he told his agent he'd no longer sign with the Yankees at the previous figures.

A day later, the Braves came in with their offer: five years and $28 million. New York made its final play and was willing to give Maddux $34 million with a $9 million signing bonus.

At 6:30 that evening, Boras called the Yankees to tell them his client was headed to Atlanta.

The Yankees pushed hard for him, with GM Gene Michael, who was with Maddux with the Cubs in the early 1980s, traveling to Las Vegas to play golf with him. He even brought Maddux to New York, showed him potential neighborhoods, and took him to a Broadway show.

In the end, the lure of what the Braves had in place, and what Maddux could add to it, won out.

"The decision for me—at the time, I was an NL player and there was an opportunity for me to go to Atlanta," Maddux said in 2014. "You've got to remember, this is 1992, too. The Braves were really good in 1991, 1992. And I had an opportunity to go there and my decision back then—I wanted to stay in the NL and I wanted the chance to be a World Series winner.

"Back then, I kind of thought Atlanta would have fit both of those needs."

Landing Maddux more than worked out in their favor. In eleven seasons, he'd go 194–88 with a 2.63 ERA, three straight Cy Youngs, 10 consecutive Gold Gloves, and six All-Star appearances before going back to Chicago in 2004.

Still, the what-ifs are tantalizing, thinking about the 620 home runs, 417 doubles, and 1,543 RBIs that Bonds would deliver from 1992 until he retired in 2007 and having them happen as a Brave.

"We would have had the best hitter in the game," Schuerholz said. "We may have won as many in a different style, a different form, a different manner.

"We may have just overwhelmed people offensively if we had Barry Bonds in the middle of our lineup for ten years, for as long as we had Greg."

*   *   *   *

Smoltz smiled as he rattled off their defined identities, as if the Big Three were the Fab Four of Paul (the cute one), George (the quiet one), Ringo (the funny one), and John (the smart one).

"Stoic Glavine. Non-emotional, not knowing what was going on," Smoltz said. "The professor, kind of the nerdy professor in Maddux . . ."

He hung there for a moment. "And then I was goofy. I just let it all hang out."

Glavine and Maddux may have had different personalities, but they approached hitters with similar tactics. While Smoltz was more of a power pitcher, they lived on the edges of the plate, changing speeds and utilizing pinpoint accuracy.

"They made it look a lot easier, at times," Smoltz said. "I know they still sweat the same way I did, but it just didn't look like it."

They were unassuming, making them a perfect foil to the burgeoning home run numbers in the 1990s, when they made an iconic Nike commercial in '98.

While crowds cheered the Cardinals' Mark McGwire putting on a show in the batting cage for a crowd that included Heather Locklear, a perturbed Glavine asked, "How long are they going to worship this guy?"

"Hey," Maddux yelled. "We've got Cy Young winners over here."

The two locked eyes before launching into a Rocky-esque montage that included them lifting weights, running stadium steps, and, after Glavine tells him "step into it," Maddux hitting his rotation mate in the stomach with a bat.

Sufficiently pumped up, they hit the cage themselves and as Glavine took a cut he drew the attention of Locklear, who called out "Hi, Tom."

The two hit their forearms in Bash Brothers fashion as Maddux stated the obvious: "Chicks dig the long ball."

That McGwire was caught up in the performance-enhancing drug scandal that would follow that era of homers comes with irony. But Glavine and Maddux's place in that ad and that catchphrase have had staying power.

"I think for both of us, we had an opportunity to do something at a fun time in baseball with the whole home run thing going on," Glavine said. "Look, Nike asks you to do a commercial? Yeah, I'm in. It was a great opportunity for us and I think, yeah, somewhere along the line, the 'Chicks dig the long ball' came from us."

Years later, Smoltz would voice some displeasure when the Big Three appeared on the MLB Network and were asked about their hitting.

Smoltz, said Maddux, had the most power at the plate, to which Smoltz replied, "I didn't get to take part in that commercial. What the heck was that?"

Hitting was a point of pride, and a competition for the trio.

"That wasn't what we got paid to do," Glavine said "but at the same time I think it was great for us, because it drove each one of us to work at it and get better at it."

Glavine won four Silver Slugger Awards and had the highest career average of the three at .186, but he went deep just once in his career, off the Reds' John Smiley in 1999. The others both hit five homers as Smoltz—a .159 hitter—delivered all of his from 1989 to 1999, while Maddux (.171 average) hit two in 1999.

"It was always about the hitting," Glavine said. "I think for us, we had so much respect for each other as pitchers and what we brought to the table that it was never a case of 'Well, I want to have a better year than you because that's going to be good for me.'"

Glavine would throw a one-hitter in Game Six of the 1995 World Series that would give the Braves their only title of the era, though that's not the game that sticks out to Mazzone as the lefty's best.

Knocked out of Game Six of the NLCS against the Pirates after just one inning in which he was burned for eight runs (seven earned) and six hits with zero strikeouts, Glavine wasn't the public's number-one choice to start the World Series opener vs. the Blue Jays.

"Everybody was saying 'How can you start Tom Glavine in Game 1 of the World Series against Toronto?'" Mazzone said. "Well, guess what, he was a 20-game winner that I recall. What's wrong with starting a 20-game winner in Game 1 of the World Series?"

Glavine answered his critics, giving up just one run and four hits in a complete game, the first of two he'd throw against the Blue Jays.

"He was bound and determined because of how he pitched against Pittsburgh in his previous start and what people were saying," Mazzone said.

It's that response that was Glavine to the core. More than anything, he wasn't going to deviate from his game plan. He refused to give in to hitters, living on the corners.

"Very good, very consistent, very stubborn, wanted to win more than the other pitcher," Maddux said.

His trademark pitch would become the circle change-up he threw with a grip he discovered by accident. He held the ball between his middle and ring fingers, forming a circle with his index finger and thumb.

Over his twenty-two-year career, Glavine would win 305 games and was amazingly durable, leading the majors in starts six times, and was in the top ten in the NL in innings pitched twelve times. He wouldn't land on the disabled list until 2008, the year he turned 42.

"He kind of taught me that you don't have to feel good to go out there and pitch and win," Maddux said. "I think everybody thinks you have to be 100 percent to go out there and compete. Even if you go out there and something is bothering you, if you've got the ball in your hand, you've got a chance to win the game."

The magic of Maddux wasn't just in the four Cy Youngs—tied with Steve Carlton for the third-most in history—the record 18 Gold Gloves, or that in the live-ball era, only Warren Spahn (363) has more wins than Maddux's 355.

It was in the way that the righty, who underscored his diminutive stature with wire-rimmed glasses, seemingly toyed with hitters.

"The thing about him was he knew a lot about hitting," said catcher Eddie Perez. "As soon as a hitter stood in there, he knew how to get him out. The way he was swinging that day, the way he was standing at home plate. It was a different game when he was out there."

Perez would know. He served as Maddux's personal catcher in Atlanta and was behind the plate for 832⅓ of his innings. When they weren't playing, part of Perez's responsibility was to sit on the bench with him, and he'd marvel at the way Maddux could predict what was going to happen.

"Sometimes he'd go, 'Well, if he throws the fastball, then it's going to be a ground ball to shortstop.' 'If he throws a slider it's going to be a hit' or whatever," Perez said. "He was always right."

The thinking-man's ace, the outfielders he played with still can't believe the way he could forecast exact plays and situations well before the game's first pitch had ever been thrown.

While going over a scouting report before they were to play Bonds and the Giants, Maddux addressed center fielder Marquis Grissom.

"I'm going to make him hit it to the warning track," Maddux told him. "I'm going to make the ball move just enough and he's going to hit it to the warning track in left-center.

"I know he can hit it out of right field, but make him hit it to left-center and you can catch it on the track."

When the time came, Maddux turned, looked at Grissom, and pointed to the left. Sure enough, Bonds made contact, but not enough, and the center fielder hauled it in on the warning track.

"Smoltzie was kind of the same way and Glavine was kind of the same way," Grissom said, "but no one was as good as Maddux at positioning his defense around him."

On April 23, 2000, Maddux approached Jordan before the game with a prediction.

"Brian, you're going to throw your first guy out at first base today from right field," he said.

"Yeah, whatever," Jordan answered.

"When [Francisco Cordova] comes up, I want you to move in," Maddux continued. "He's going to hit a bullet between first and second and you just be you in the outfield."

Sure enough, when Cordova came up, Maddux shot Jordan a look and a nod. The right fielder moved in and Cordova hit a line drive between first and second. Jordan picked up the ball and fired it to first base for the out. Maddux tipped his hat in recognition.

"I was just like 'This guy is the best ever,'" Jordan said.

There are countless stories from countless players, all of them left stunned at his perceived ability to see exactly how a play would unfold.

"Aw, for every time it happened, there's probably fifty times it didn't," he said.

Maddux had a walk rate of 1.8 per nine innings, the fifth lowest ever among pitchers with at least 3,000 innings, and he's the only pitcher with 300 wins, 3,000 strikeouts, and fewer than 1,000 walks.

"Good control makes you smart," he said. "You throw the ball where you want to throw it, you look smart."

While he could run his fastball to 90 mph, Maddux lived in the 85–87 range, producing a misdirection that he attributed to just the smallest changes in pressure in his grip.

"It's like playing Wiffle Ball in the backyard," said Boggs, who went 1-for-13 (.077) vs. Maddux. "The ball . . . it moved all over the place. It started in, and [would] run over the plate; it started in and cut in on your hands. That's exactly what people ask me, 'What was it like?' It was like playing Wiffle Ball in the backyard. . . . He wasn't a lot of fun to face."

But to watch was a different story. Even Glavine picked up tips, like how a hitter reacted to a pitch they took or how they would foul one off.

"You'd go to the ballpark wondering how efficient he was going to be carving up the opponent," Glavine said. "He did things so efficiently, so methodically."

The antithesis of Glavine's and Maddux's calm, cool presences on the mound was Smoltz. He was fire, both in his arsenal and the emotion he played with.

"[People] felt like I gave everything I had every time I pitched and that's kind of what I felt like," Smoltz said. "I had fun. I learned to know the difference between having fun and being serious at the moment and people saw that.

"I was not afraid to show my emotions, but at the same time I learned how to handle my emotions. Easier said than done, because early on I didn't do a very good job."

The control of his pitches haunted him for much of his early career, leading the league in wild pitches in 1990 (14), 1991 (20), and 1992 (17), but it was that turnaround from 2–11 in '91 that helped start the Braves' run of division titles as Cox stuck with him.

"My belief has always been if you're good enough to come up—and we liked him down in the minor leagues a lot—you've got to give them time," Cox said. "There's going to be some down times, believe me, in the major leagues, either as a hitter or pitcher.

"I love sticking with people and I've stuck with a lot of people that really succeeded when people didn't think they would."

With Mazzone, Smoltz worked on a four-seam slider that would become the stuff of his legend. Averaging 86 mph, it came out of his hand looking like a fastball, but broke away from right-handed hitters. Over his career, righties hit just .216 against him.

"I realized what a weapon it was and the luxury it had against right-handers," Smoltz said.

"Let's face it," former Braves catcher Greg Olson told the *Atlanta Journal-Constitution*, "he had one of the best, if not the best, tight sliders in the game. That was his out pitch; that was his strikeout pitch."

In twenty years, the final of which—2009—he played with the Red Sox and Cardinals, Smoltz made eight All-Star teams and won the 1996 Cy Young. He would lead the NL in wins, innings, and strikeouts and won 14 or more games 10 times.

Smoltz's legacy, though, rested in his versatility.

"There wasn't a pitch invented that he couldn't throw," Maddux said. "I've seen him throw a circle-change, splits, knuckleballs, curves. I mean, he threw every pitch in the book and he could learn it quickly and he threw it well."

Smoltz began throwing the knuckleball in 1999 to ease the pain he was feeling in his elbow. He would ultimately need Tommy John surgery at age 34, causing him to miss the entire 2000 season. It was one of five procedures he'd undergo in his career (four on his elbow and another on his shoulder).

Smoltz transitioned to the bullpen in his return from Tommy John, going on to save 154 games as a closer and becoming a three-time All-Star in the role. He is the only pitcher with at least 200 wins and more than 150 saves.

"For him to be as good as he was at two different roles: starter and closer, was pretty unique," Glavine said, "and I think it says a lot about his ability and his mentality that he was able to do both roles so well."

In 2005 Smoltz moved back to the rotation and was again an All-Star, starting 33 games at age 38. The following season he led the majors with 35 starts.

"If I truly wanted to make the Hall of Fame, selfishly, I would have never left the bullpen," Smoltz said. "I just would have stayed there and probably gotten who knows how many more saves? I was not about that."

Smoltz thrived on the biggest stage, his 15 postseason wins ranking second all-time behind Andy Pettitte's 19. In his 27 playoff starts he gave up two runs or less 18 times.

"If you wanted to win a big game, there was nobody better to put up there," Glavine said. "He was phenomenal in those types of settings."

After surgery on his right shoulder, he signed with the Red Sox in '09. The numbers weren't pretty, as the 42-year-old had an 8.32 ERA and 2–5 record.

Designated for assignment, he cleared waivers and joined St. Louis. In his debut he set a franchise record by striking out seven straight, but he'd go 1–3 with a 4.26 ERA in the regular season.

His final game came in Game Three of that year's NLDS as he threw two innings of relief, giving up an earned run on four hits.

Smoltz was the longest tenured of the Big Three, spending twenty years in Atlanta, but Glavine was the only one to end his career in a Braves uniform.

John Smoltz donned a wig during his Hall of Fame speech in 2015 as payback for comments Tom Glavine and Greg Maddux made the year before. (*Arturo Pardavila III*)

The first of the group to leave when he joined the division rival Mets in 2002—where he would join the 300-win club—Glavine stayed there for five seasons before turning to Atlanta in 2008. His return ended with that first DL stint as he'd have surgery on his left elbow and shoulder.

Glavine attempted to come back for his twenty-third season, signing a one-year deal with the Braves, but he was released while on a rehab assignment in the minors.

Maddux moved on the year after Glavine joined the Mets, returning to the Cubs for parts of three seasons before stints with the Dodgers and Padres.

In 2008 he stood at a podium at the annual Winter Meetings in his hometown of Las Vegas and announced his retirement.

As expected, he kept his composure.

"Mad Dog threw a shutout today," Cox told reporters. "Special, special guy. I get choked up talking about him."

There was little Glavine, Maddux, and Smoltz didn't accomplish, as teammates or individuals—except for one thing.

Twice while the three pitchers were together, the Braves had no-nos—but it was Kent Mercker that started in both of them, teaming with relievers Mark Wohlers and Pena on September 11, 1991 vs. the Padres, and solo in April 8, 1994, no-hitting the Dodgers.

Glavine and Smoltz threw seven one-hitters each, with four of Glavine's coming in Atlanta, while Maddux threw nine in his career. Seven of those were when he was a Brave.

But with the mind games Maddux liked to play with hitters, Perez says a no-hitter may have defeated the purpose.

"Even umpires would ask me, 'Hey, has he ever thrown a no-hitter?'" the catcher said. "I told them, 'I don't think he wants to throw a no-hitter.'"

★   ★   ★   ★

President Jimmy Carter has a photo of himself, Glavine, Maddux, and Smoltz, POTUS showing the trio "how to hold a baseball properly," he said. Being an unabashed Braves fan, it could come off as hyperbole when he puts them in historical context, calling the Big Three "the most outstanding pitching staff, maybe, that baseball's ever seen."

Three plaques in the Baseball Hall of Fame, and a combined seven Cy Youngs, all by pitchers whose heydays were in Atlanta, say the Peanut Farmer wasn't wrong.

Stoic. Calculated. Fiery. The characteristics of the Braves' Big Three made them different, but there's no separating them. Not ever.

"It's just great knowing that whenever anyone talks about the Braves, the three of us are in the conversation," Glavine said.

From the left: Tom Glavine and Greg Maddux entered the Hall of Fame with their manager, Bobby Cox, in 2014. (*Arturo Pardavila III*)

Chapter Eight

Team and Stadium Catch Fire

That's a problem, Joe Simpson thought as he calmly looked across Atlanta–Fulton County Stadium and saw smoke billowing out of the hospitality area next to the radio booth.

Moments later, flames followed and Simpson then realized something.

"You know what?" he said to himself. "I better go get my briefcase."

As he had done so many times before, Simpson had taken his briefcase to the radio booth—located on one end of press row—and made his way back to the television booth that was located on the opposite side.

In those days, the TBS and Braves Radio Network analysts would start on one medium and end on the other, and on July 20, 1993, Simpson and Skip Caray would start on TV and end their night on the radio.

Simpson, as was his routine, was going over his pre-game notes and writing names into the lineup card when he heard talk of smoke. When he could see fire, he was certain that when it was put out, his briefcase would be soaked.

A former outfielder and first baseman with the Dodgers, Mariners, and Royals before his retirement ten years earlier, Simpson ran toward the radio booth, put his hand over his nose and mouth, reached inside the opening into the room, grabbed his bag, and ran.

"I'm glad I didn't wait any longer than I did to go get it," said Simpson, who currently serves as an analyst on FOX Sports South and FOX Sports Southeast telecasts.

People began pouring out of the press box as the smoke continued to grow thicker and thicker.

"You hear about it, but you don't realize how fast rooms fill up with smoke and you're trying to stay low," Simpson said.

By the time he had taken the elevator from the con-course to the field and emerged in the dugout, the press box had erupted in flames.

"The whole thing was on fire. The flames were belch-ing out of the front of the radio booth and that hospitality booth," Simpson said. "It didn't take long at all for it to become completely engulfed."

Simpson had his briefcase, but Rick Hummel didn't have time to grab his computer.

The *St. Louis Post-Dispatch* Cardinals beat writer was working on pregame content, and while the flames were visible from field level, "I was upstairs, virtually oblivious to all of it," he said.

Finally, he heard someone down below yell "GET OUT!" and could smell the fire. He bolted from the press box—the last one to leave—but in the rush, he had left his computer behind.

"People told me later how stupid I looked up there, Rome is burning, but I was so immersed in my silliness of work I didn't know what was going on," he said.

As for his computer, it would be fine, though it was charred a little bit.

"It didn't work much longer," Hummel said.

Braves pitcher Tom Glavine was watching film to prepare for that night's start when he "Heard there was a little fire," he said. "I came up and—Oh, my God—that was more than a little fire."

It came ninety minutes before the second of the three-game series against the Cardinals, starting in an empty suite being rented by Atlanta radio station News Radio 640 AM WGST on the third-base side. A can of Sterno, which was used to keep food warm, spilled. Smoke immediately filled the area, and once fire extinguishers were found, it couldn't be contained.

Early-arriving fans had been evacuated, but batting practice continued as normal, at least for a while.

"Players are kind of immune to stuff like that," Hummel said. "I don't remember anyone being tragically nervous."

Braves second baseman Jeff Blauser found some humor in the situation, talking to a CNN camera as he strolled across the field, the fire raging behind him. "Might have been what it looked like when Sherman rolled through town," he said, referencing William Tecumseh Sherman's siege of Atlanta in 1864 in which he ordered military resources be burned. The fire left the city in ruins.

Blauser did go into a more somber tone as he said, "I don't know. It's unfortunate. I hope nobody's stuck up there. I hope everybody's safe. Sometimes this puts the game in perspective. Some things are more important than this game."

An explosion was heard as beams burst above the box and debris fell onto the field-level suites below. The fire burned for twenty-five minutes before firefighters would be able to draw close enough to put it out.

"I just ran out onto the field and looked up and it scared the hell out of me," St. Louis manager Joe Torre told reporters. "I just kept running into the outfield."

Firefighters had initially tried to attack it from outside the stadium, but due to a lack of a direct route, had to go onto the field via a tunnel. They pulled hoses through the outside ramps to get to the club level where the suite was located. TV cameras captured the surreal scene as a fire truck pulled out onto the playing surface to allow them to fight the flames from both sides.

"The tough thing about firefighting this fire was that they have ramps, they don't have stairs," assistant fire chief Larry Tanner told the Associated Press. "So we had to run a hundred feet one way and then a hundred feet the other way to get up to the next level."

The result was $1.5 million in damages, as five suites had been destroyed and a sixth was harmed, and the stadium's public-address system was left inoperable. A firefighter was treated for smoke inhalation, but no other injuries were reported.

All the while, players and media from both sides watched it all unfold.

This can't be happening, Simpson thought. *Are you serious? Nobody's ever seen anything like this before in a ballpark.*

As Simpson stood with a group of players he was approached by Jane Fonda, who was then the wife of Braves and TBS owner Ted Turner.

"Oh my gosh, that's right," she said to Simpson as the radio booth burned. "That's where you work."

But not that night; of that Simpson was certain. "I just figured, 'Yeah, we're done,'" he said.

Hall of Fame Cardinals announcer Jack Buck echoed those sentiments as he joked to CNN: "I could see it spread and I knew that we would be fired out of the game. I've been rained out. I've been snowed out. I've been cold out. I've been fired, but not fired out of a ball game."

Turner, though, had other plans.

He walked up to general manager John Schuerholz, who was in a group with Blauser, shortstop Mark Lemke, team president Stan Kasten, and the fire marshal, and said "Tonight, Atlanta–Fulton County Stadium caught on fire, and so too will the Braves."

The show would go on.

TBS producer Glenn Diamond told Simpson, "You know what? Ted wants this game to be played. He wants us to be on the air. He wants to show how we can persevere here and we can overcome any adversity and we'll get this done."

Turner got the okay of marshals, who had deemed the 28-year-old stadium structurally safe, though 2,000 seats were roped off.

Booth assistants began setting up tables in a section of seats next to the press box, folding the legs down and draping them across the backs of chairs. Instead of press row separating them, the radio and television teams would now be sitting next to each other.

"Skip said 'This is pretty neat,'" Simpson recalled. "'We're going to get this on the air,' and he loved challenges, so this was definitely a hell of a challenge."

Reporters were moved to folding chairs behind them, each given a makeshift mask to safeguard from any after-effects of the smoke.

"They weren't exactly like you'd get at some great hospital," said Hummel, who was the only St. Louis writer there, joined by a handful of reporters from the *Atlanta Journal-Constitution.* "Someone just kind of constructed them, I think."

At 9:20 p.m., fans were allowed back into the stadium, and at 9:38 p.m., two hours after originally scheduled, the teams were playing.

"It was crazy," Simpson said.

The show went on. Broadcasting despite the disaster may have largely been Turner wanting to persevere, but there was also the fact that he had a brand-new weapon to put on display.

Fred McGriff.

"I'm just worried there's going to be too much pressure on the guy," Blauser told the New York *Daily News* before the first baseman, who the Braves had acquired in a deal with the Padres, made it to the stadium. "His arrival here is a big deal because he can help out a lot. But it isn't fair to expect him to be the difference between second and first place."

In his first game in a Braves uniform, the first baseman would dig into the batter's box in the sixth inning to face the Cardinals' Rene Arocha, who had already gotten him to ground out to first base twice.

Coming into that at-bat, McGriff was 1-for-5 against Arocha on the season, with that lone hit a single. But on the first pitch, McGriff reached out and clubbed a fastball on the outside part of the plate, connecting on a two-run home run to tie the game at 5–5.

Nicknamed the Crime Dog, à la McGruff, the cartoon dog that was used to build crime awareness among children—his motto: "Take a bite out of crime!" —McGriff was greeted by an Atlanta fan holding aloft a sign that read "Fire Dog McGriff" as he made his way around the bases.

"He could run for mayor tomorrow and win," sportscaster Pete Van Wieren said as McGriff strode back toward the dugout.

"Or fire marshal tonight," Sutton added, "and win that in a landslide."

After all that had happened to McGriff before the game, including traveling 400 miles from his Florida home (an eight-hour drive he fit into six), it left McGriff to summarize it all succinctly. "With the fire and driving from Tampa—what a day," he told reporters. "I need some sleep."

Says Simpson as he recalls McGriff's blast, "That made it even more memorable and it was just . . . I'll say it was an exciting night, to say the least and certainly not your normal run-of-the-mill game in July."

It was Sid Bream who lost his spot in the lineup to McGriff, and if anyone was thinking he was responsible, he went on the offensive with tongue firmly planted in cheek.

"It was very ironic that the day Freddy comes into the place that that takes place," Bream said. "I know I said that 'I didn't do it. I promise I didn't do it.'"

While the fire raged before the game, McGriff was trying to get in some work in the indoor batting cage, but security ordered him out while the fire raged.

"What a start," McGriff would say.

He had no idea.

The Braves claimed McGriff's debut 8–5, his homer completing a rally as they entered the sixth inning down 5–0. He would smack two more home runs the next game, and fourteen over his first forty-eight games. The spark he provided helped the Braves chase down the Giants, who had a 9½ game lead in the West when McGriff arrived in Atlanta.

"We caught on fire and had an historical, remarkable end of season run," Schuerholz said.

McGriff had a big follow-through, a motion in which the lefty released with his dominant hand and let the bat twirl back in his extended right arm in a helicopter finish. It was unique, an epic swoop that McGriff had pieced together early in his career.

He had read *The Art of Hitting .300* by Royals hitting coach Charley Lau (with Alfred Glossbrenner) and began focusing on finishing high. After signing with the Blue Jays, manager Cito Gaston helped McGriff to add a weight shift through his swing, and when McGriff would attempt to swing down on the ball, the bat would end back behind his head.

"I try to finish high to get that extension and the carry on the ball," he said in a video from his playing days. "I try to swing down and make good contact."

The 6-foot-3, 200-pounder had hit 209 home runs by July 11, 2013, spending four full seasons in Toronto and 2½ in San Diego. From 1988 to 1992 he had hit an average of 34 per season, including 36 for the Jays in '89 to lead the American League. Then, three years later, he topped the NL as a Padre with 35, making him the first player in the modern era to claim the HR crown in each league.

McGriff was simply one of the few bright spots for San Diego, which was 26 games back in the NL West at 33–56, but he was also expensive for a team looking to unload payroll.

The Padres had already shed Gary Sheffield's $3.11 million contract, shipping him to the Marlins, and the 29-year-old McGriff was making the most of anyone on the roster at $4 million. In dealing him, San Diego would stand to trim more than $12 million from its Opening Day 1992 payroll.

"From what they've been telling me, it's basically money," McGriff told the AP. "I never thought it would get to the day where I made too much money and it became a bad situation."

While they still had perennial All-Star Tony Gwynn, San Diego was looking to add youth to build around him, getting minor leaguers Andres Berumen, Trevor Hoffman—the future saves king—and Jose Martinez for Sheffield.

It was all part of a movement that was a point of contention in San Diego, as they dealt Darrin Jackson to the Blue Jays on March 30, a trade that came after the team sent season-ticket holders a letter saying they would be contenders due to players like Jackson. Two fans filed a class-action suit that was settled out of court five days before McGriff was shipped to Atlanta.

Schuerholz was more than happy to help with those rebuilding efforts as the Braves offense was ailing. Hitting a collective .246, which ranked last in the NL, they were scoring 4.07 runs per game, putting them third from the bottom in the majors.

While they had Ron Gant and David Justice—both of whom hit 20 home runs in the first half of the '93 season—they were getting little to no power at first base from the platoon of Bream and Brian Hunter. Bream, who started against left-handers, was hitting .239 with eight homers, and Brian Hunter, the pick vs. righties, had a .132 average and zero HRs.

"It was a recognition of the fact that if we didn't get a cleanup hitter all of our guys up and down our lineup—who tried to become more than they were, tried to make up for the fact that we didn't have a fourth-place hitter hitting 30-plus home runs and driving in 100-plus runs—they all tried to do more than they could," Schuerholz said. "They came out of their comfort zones and it was a mismatch and it was hard to watch."

McGriff had been linked to the Braves for weeks, but the two sides couldn't agree on a package.

"I just kept grinding and grinding and calling and calling and talking and talking and negotiating the package and so on and so forth until we got to one where they finally said 'Yes,'" Schuerholz said. "I said 'no' enough times and they said 'no' enough times and we finally settled on a package that worked for us."

Atlanta refused to include prospects Chipper Jones or Javy Lopez, who were hitting over .300 at the time for Triple-A Richmond. Ryan Klesko was included in a number of reported deals, but ultimately, Schuerholz managed to hold on to all three.

"It was important for us to keep Ryan in the organization," Schuerholz told Knight-Ridder News Service. "That was one of the reasons it took as long as it did."

Atlanta would send Triple-A outfielder Melvin Nieves and pitcher Donnie Elliott and Single-A outfielder Vince Moore to the Padres for McGriff and an undisclosed amount of money.

"It's like playing poker where you have four aces and, all of a sudden, someone hands you a fifth," Justice would later tell the *Sun-Sentinel*.

Nieves appeared in 127 games over three seasons in San Diego, and in his most productive season, 1994, when he played in 98 games, he hit just .205/.276./.419 with 14 homers and 38 RBIs. Meanwhile, Elliott had a 3.27 ERA with 24 strikeouts and 21 walks over 33 innings in 30 games in '94 and pitched just once in '95 before he was released, and Moore never progressed past Double A.

Established in 1986, the July 31 non-waiver trade deadline has produced some massive deals in its thirty years of existence.

There were those that paid immediate dividends.

Nomar Garciaparra went from Boston to the Cubs in 2004—a move that sparked the Red Sox to go 34–12 en route to their first World Series in eighty-six years—and Manny Ramirez headed to the Dodgers in 2008 in a three-team deal with the Red Sox and Pirates. The mercurial outfielder would go on to hit .396 with 17 HRs and 53 RBIs in helping Los Angeles capture the West crown.

Likewise, the Brewers got C. C. Sabathia the same year as the Ramirez trade and he pitched 130⅔ innings in eighty-three days in the regular season, throwing seven complete games with three shutouts while propelling Milwaukee to the postseason.

Some trades included massive stars, including sending future Hall of Famer John Smoltz from the Tigers to Atlanta in '87, Randy Johnson from the Mariners to the Astros in '98, Mark McGwire from the Athletics to the Cardinals in '97, and Curt Schilling from the Phillies to the Diamondbacks in '00.

Trades would set themselves up for future scrutiny, like the 2007 swap that saw the Braves acquire Mark Teixeira, a trade that would take on a more infamous tone given what Atlanta gave up and that they flipped him a year later to the Angels.

Getting Schilling ultimately helped propel Arizona to a title in 2001, but those other deals would lose their luster.

Ramirez had one more productive season in Los Angeles before his suspension for using a fertility drug, and Johnson, Sabathia, and Teixeira all left as free agents in the offseason after those trades. McGwire's time in St. Louis did help save baseball after the 1994 strike, but that run would be tainted by steroids use.

The Smoltz deal would ultimately weigh heavily in the Braves' favor, but let's not forget the Tigers got what they wanted too, as Doyle Alexander proved crucial in their AL East title push.

It's the McGriff deal, though, that stands as one of the most lopsided in the deadline's history because Schuerholz not only obtained a player in his prime, who would go on to be a catalyst in '93 and beyond, but also got him for a trio that would fade into obscurity.

Without question, it is the GM's signature trade.

But Schuerholz doesn't look at deals from the end of who won or who lost; he sees them in terms of motivation and the Padres' vision was clear.

"What they're looking at it is not how much it helps the Braves, but how much this trade helps them," Schuerholz said. "That's the primary perspective. Secondary, they may say, 'Well, we don't want to help the Braves. It's obnoxious how much they win and how often they win. We don't want to do that.' But first concern is do what's best for your organization and your team."

McGriff would stick around for four-plus seasons in Atlanta, hitting 130 home runs with 446 RBIs. He made three consecutive All-Star Games from 1994 to 1996 and was eighth in the MVP voting in '94 when he had his finest season, with a career-best 1.012 OPS, supplying 34 homers and 107 RBIs.

During the 1995 World Series he delivered home runs in Games One and Three, and in 45 postseason games with the Braves, McGriff hit .323 with 10 homers and 34 RBIs. His .992 OPS is the second-highest for any first baseman since 1993 appearing in more than 16 playoff games, trailing only Albert Pujols's 1.039 in 70 games.

But maybe McGriff's biggest impact was what he meant to those around him in the lineup.

After he joined the Braves, hitting .310 with 19 home runs and 55 RBIs with a 1.004 OPS in 68 games, he elevated number three hitter Gant, as well as Justice, who hit fourth.

Gant would finish the year with 36 home runs and 120 RBIs, with 16 homers and 62 of those runs coming after McGriff's arrival. Justice hit 19 more homers and added 59 more RBIs, giving him 40 HRs and 120 RBIs on the season.

"When he came over, it all sort of clicked," center fielder and leadoff hitter Otis Nixon told the *Daily News*.

Nixon also took off after the deal, with a .300 average compared to .237 before McGriff. "There was a positive reaction, as if now we can really do something."

There were casualties, as Bream made just two starts the rest of the season. Primarily used as a pinch hitter, he had 40 plate appearances in 36 games, and would leave for the Astros as a free agent that winter.

Hunter was demoted to the minors after McGriff was acquired and would be dealt to the Pirates that offseason.

"Obviously when you don't have an opportunity to be the main guy at first base or whatever it takes a little bit of wind out of your sails," Bream said. "I still provided them with quite a few key pinch hits that year after Fred came."

It wasn't all McGriff, as the Braves went 18–10 before the All-Star break and Gant hit twice in a game three times before the deal. But he was without question the catalyst.

The Braves went 51–17, scoring 5.8 runs per game after averaging four previously, and claimed 14 of the 16 games in which he homered. They also led the NL with 169 homers and hit at least three in a game 10 times following the deal.

Greg Maddux, who would go on to win that year's Cy Young, was 12–2 in 16 second-half starts after missing the All-Star Game with a 8–8 record in which he received two runs or less 11 times, hampering his 2.83 ERA.

Likewise, Steve Avery went from a 3.25 ERA before McGriff to 2.55 after him, and John Smoltz jumped from eight wins to 15 in five fewer starts than he had in the first half.

Glavine's record didn't show much change, as he was 11–4 before July 20 and 11–2 after, but he received three runs or less of backing nine times prior to McGriff. After, the Braves scored at least four runs in 14 of his next 16 outings.

"I don't think you can overemphasize Freddie as a catalyst," Maddux told the *Daily News*. "Freddie's been a tremendous hitter for us since the day he arrived here."

On October 3, a crowd of nearly 4,000 watched the Giants and Dodgers on Atlanta-County Stadium's big screen. The leftovers from a crowd of 48,904 that saw the Braves drop the Rockies 5–3 in the regular-season finale, they were waiting to see if the road to the playoffs would last one more day.

Despite their 103 victories, the Giants had to win to force a one-game playoff, and a charter had been scheduled to take the Braves to San Francisco.

They wouldn't need it.

Mike Piazza, the NL Rookie of the Year, hit two home runs as the Dodgers steamrolled their rivals 12–1. The Braves had completed their epic comeback. Down 10 games on July 22, Atlanta claimed 22 of its last 29.

"You couldn't afford to lose and neither of us ever seemed to," manager Bobby Cox told the *Los Angeles Times*.

The Braves would go on to lose that National League Championship Series to the Phillies 4–2, dropping the last three games.

McGriff continued his tear in that series, going 10 for 27 (.435) with a homer and four RBIs, but overall the offense went flat, managing a combined seven runs in the losses.

Throughout the run, McGriff had deflected credit for his undeniable impact. Though in the midst of the champagne bottles popping after the Braves clinched the division, he did give way to one moment of reflection.

"When I come out with my book, this will be it— 'Worst to First . . . In Two Months,'" McGriff told the *Atlanta Journal-Constitution*.

Chapter Nine

Crowned, At Last

Little Mama had a premonition—the sight of a ball falling into a glove in center field—and in the third inning of Game Six of the 1995 World Series, the security guard sought out the man from her vision to share it with him.

Marquis Grissom had met Little Mama in April, the center fielder having been traded to Atlanta from the Expos in a four-player deal three weeks before the start of the season. When he had arrived at the stadium, he saw a guard talking to everyone who passed.

"I said, 'Hey there shorty, how you doing?'" Grissom recalled. "And she lit into my ass."

"He called me 'shorty' and I was like 'Who in the hell are you calling 'shorty?'" said that longtime guard, Faye Perry. "You're no skyscraper yourself."

"I'll just call you Little Mama," the amused 5-foot-11 outfielder replied.

And so it went: Little Mama approached the player she referred to as Griss, and on that cool October night at Atlanta–Fulton County Stadium, told him: "You can let me have that ball when you catch the final out."

If Grissom bought into her prediction, though, he wasn't showing.

"My thing was, 'Okay, all right, he doesn't believe me,'" Perry said.

The Braves were leading 1–0, one out from the city of Atlanta's first title in any sport, when the Indians' Carlos Baerga bit on the first offering from closer Mark Wohlers and floated it toward left-center field.

"I had that feeling that he was going to get that ball because he was out there in center field and I was like, 'If anybody was to catch the ball and it goes up high, then Marquis would be the one to get it,'" Perry said.

A running Grissom tracked it down, the ball falling toward him, and everything slowed down. The Atlanta native thought of his parents, his children, and his teachers—and he kept running as he made the catch, his hands outstretched.

"Those are the things that went through my mind," Grissom said. "It was the most rewarding feeling in the world to be a champion here in Atlanta."

But he didn't forget Little Mama.

Amid the celebration, the bench clearing to join in on the dog pile on the mound—with Wohlers, third baseman Chipper Jones, and catcher Javy Lopez at the bottom—and the hugs, Grissom sought out the security guard.

"I'll take the trophy and the win," he told her.

The ball? That was hers.

"Are you serious?" Perry said as Grissom autographed it before handing it over.

"Just by her predicting that we were going to win, but not only that, that I would catch the final out . . . it was just automatic for me to give her that ball," Grissom said.

Grissom's catch sealed that crowning moment for the team of the 1990s—who had failed in their previous two trips to the World Series—and proved a security guard part Nostradamus. But it was Tom Glavine and David Justice that put them in those positions to begin with.

✳　　✳　　✳　　✳

I f opponents were going to get to Glavine, chances are it was coming in the first inning.

Throughout his Hall of Fame career, the lefty struggled in that frame with a 4.58 ERA, which was nearly half a run higher than any other inning, and it was even more of a problem in 1995. He posted a 7.76 ERA in 29 games in the first, compared to 0.93 an inning later.

"My first inning problems are well-chronicled and I never really knew what was going to happen when I got out there," he said.

So when he had a great warmup session ahead of Game Six vs. Cleveland, he didn't think anything of it. He had many experiences when things felt great before the game, then he'd end up having to use that opening inning to get himself back on track.

Add in the gravity of the situation—the 29-year-old had pitched in just one division clincher in the regular season and never thrown that late into a World Series, getting the Game Two and Five assignments in 1991, Games One and Four in 1992. He had already pitched the second game, a 4–3 Braves win over the Indians.

In those three early-Series assignments, Glavine's ERA stood at 1.57, but in Game Five against the Twins in 1991 and Game Four vs. the Blue Jays a year later, he was at 3.38.

"I didn't take anything for granted," Glavine said. "I just wanted to go out there, have a clean inning, and get off the field and get myself off to a good start."

Not that he needed any further motivation with a title on the line, but if it came, it could be traced to that season's Cy Young Award winner—and the winner of the three before that—rotation mate Greg Maddux.

With an opportunity to end the series in Cleveland, Maddux was roughed up in Game Five. Having won 18 straight decisions on the road, he gave up four earned runs on seven hits with three walks. The Braves still led 3–2, but had that game altered the landscape of the series?

"They've lost the last two World Series they've been in," Orel Hershiser, who was on the mound for the Indians in Game Five, would say. "Atlanta fans are probably wondering what is going on."

The Braves' reaction?

"Orel should keep his mouth shut," manager Bobby Cox told reporters. "He can play his games with babies somewhere. We're all grown-ups over here."

Maddux and Glavine rode together to Atlanta–Fulton County Stadium from their Alpharetta homes during an off-day workout, and Maddux talked of fitting endings. Of the staff's core, Glavine had been there the longest, having been drafted by Atlanta in 1984 and making his debut in 1987 at age 21. He suffered 17 losses in 1988 and won 20 games in both '91 and '92 when the Braves watched someone else celebrate a title. He was also the one who took the heat as one of the central figures during the 1994–1995 strike, appearing on national TV to defend the players' side of the labor dispute, and he was often booed at home in 1995 because of it.

So, as Maddux saw it, while he couldn't deliver, there was no one else who should be on the mound for a game that gave the Braves their first title in Atlanta.

"It's funny, I was thinking the very same thing about him the night before because of the season he had," Glavine told the *Atlanta Journal-Constitution*. "What Greg said really made me feel good. Certainly, this is a unique opportunity. It's what it's all about."

Grissom saw a difference in Glavine as they prepared for that night. While he had success against the Indians' offense in that previous start, holding them to two earned runs on five hits over six innings, Glavine had an undeniable edge about him.

"We had confidence in all three of those guys, [John Smoltz], Glavine and Maddux, we always knew we had the upper hand because it's going to be tough to beat those three guys three games in a row," Grissom said. "But Tommy, Tommy for some reason, had this attitude that he wanted the game, that he wanted to do it then."

Glavine got the fast start he wanted, getting Kenny Lofton to pop out to right-center field, followed by a swinging strikeout by Omar Vizquel and Baerga's groundout to first base. But more importantly, what he felt in his pregame work had translated into the game itself.

"When I walked off that mound in the first inning, the feeling that I had was 'Okay, what I had in the bullpen I just brought with me out here and that's a good sign,'" he said.

He didn't let up, allowing just two baserunners through the first five innings, both of which were Albert Belle. The left fielder was second in the American League MVP voting behind the Red Sox's Mo Vaughn, after hitting an MLB-high 50 homers and tying for first in doubles (52) and second in RBIs (126).

Glavine walked him on four pitches in the second inning, then battled for nine pitches in the fifth. But he and the Braves ended any threat, as Lopez caught Belle stealing with Eddie Murray at bat before Glavine struck

Murray and Manny Ramirez out. The Indians couldn't get anything going in the fifth inning either, as Murray followed Belle with a popout before Ramirez replaced Belle at first on a fielder's choice to shortstop Mark Lemke. Glavine fanned Jim Thome to end the inning.

"As the game went on and built up I felt more and more in command and better and better about what I was doing," Glavine said. "Again, I didn't get too far ahead of myself, because that was a really good team. That was the best offensive lineup I ever pitched against in my career."

He stressed that last part is no cliché, and the numbers back him up. Cleveland led the majors in runs (840), home runs (207), batting average (.291), and on-base (.361) and slugging (.479) percentages during that regular season. The potential for that group at a place known as the Launching Pad was devastating—and Glavine held them hitless through five innings.

"He just carved us up," said then–Indians general manager John Hart. "We had a great offense, I mean we were a 1,000-run team [including the postseason], we won 100 games in 144, I mean it was phenomenal. He cut us up."

Hart had seen enough of Glavine before to know what he was capable of. When Hart was still on the field, serving as Triple-A Rochester's manager in the Orioles' system in 1986 and 1987, he faced Glavine, then with the Braves' International League team in Richmond.

"You could see that Glavine was going to be good," Hart said. "He wasn't there yet. He didn't have the change-up, didn't have the command yet."

The Glavine he saw in the World Series was at the height of his powers, winning 91 games between 1991 and 1995—one more than Maddux—and had made three straight All-Star teams and claimed two Silver Sluggers.

Hart joked that afterward he addressed the pitches Glavine was getting with home plate umpire Joe Brinkman, saying "Man, that was the widest strike zone I ever saw."

The former-Cleveland GM jokes now, but at the time it was a heated topic as Glavine parked his trademark changeup on the outside corner inning after inning. Murray took exception, debating with Brinkman, as did Vizquel.

This was Glavine at his finest: pinpoint location, deception, switching speeds. He had thrown 76 pitches through five, facing one batter over the minimum, while counterpart Dennis Martinez sat at 90. It wasn't until Tony Pena's soft single to right field to lead off the sixth inning that the Indians would get their first—and only—hit.

Only nine pitchers in World Series history have thrown one-hitters, and while the Yankees' Orlando Hernandez and David Cone would both do so at the Braves' expense in 1999, Glavine's was the first since the Red Sox' Jim Lonborg in 1967.

"He pitched," Hart said. "Nothing was overpowering, his fastball was average, threw his changeup any count he wanted to, mixed in his breaking ball, painted the corners, got a lot of strikes off the corners that were outside. He got a lot of those."

After Pena reached in the sixth, Indians manager Mike Hargrove let reliever Jim Poole—a six-year veteran who had yet to record a major-league at-bat—hit.

The logic in keeping the southpaw reliever in to bat was that the Braves would hit two lefties to start the sixth (David Justice and Ryan Klesko) and in all, left-handed hitters had a collective .211 average against Poole in the regular season.

But Poole's bunt attempt resulted in a foul popout to first baseman Fred McGriff, and while Lofton reached on a fielder's-choice grounder and subsequently stole second, he was stranded there by a Vizquel fly out to first.

Glavine marched into the Atlanta dugout and angrily proclaimed, "Just get me one, because they're not getting any."

"Whoa," said pitching coach Leo Mazzone as he turned to manager Bobby Cox.

"You hear that, Leo?" Cox asked.

"Yeah."

"That's awesome, isn't it," Cox replied.

It was, more than anything, the anti-Glavine moment. His stoic demeanor was as much part of his makeup as that changeup. Lemke, the lefty's roommate when they were together at rookie ball in Bradenton, recalls that even then "he always has his head on right, was always a little more mature than the rest of us."

That approach worked with a game where he was working to bend a strike zone to his will and it worked in labor negotiations. "His composure on the mound, it's similar to the way he carries himself," said Kevin Young, the Pirates' player rep, during those talks. "There aren't a lot of people who can really lead. The way he goes about it, dealing with these issues, he carries the same intensity and image. The total image."

Glavine's outburst as he bounded into that dugout was something very different, but it was that kind of night.

"It was a little bit bravado, a little bit confidence in myself," Glavine said. "Look, I'm not going to lie, I was feeling it. I knew I was pitching good and for me it was more about firing the guys up offensively than me really believing that."

It's a declaration that grew in legend, but David Justice admits he wasn't even aware it happened.

"I never knew that," he said. "But that's all he needed. I didn't know that."

Justice had drawn the ire of Atlanta fans ahead of Game Six, venting for 15 minutes—unprompted, mind you—about what he perceived as a lack of enthusiasm after the way the Jacobs Field crowd reacted to the Indians' 5–4 win in Game Five. He even alluded to a touch of expectation, with the Braves' playing in their third World Series in five years.

"If we don't win, they'll probably burn our houses down," Justice told reporters. "We've got to win. And if we win, it's for the twenty-five guys in here, the coaches and Bobby [Cox]. It is for us. Like the song '[You and me] Against the World.' It's us against the world. I'm the only guy that will sit here and say it, but there are a lot of people that feel this way."

He continued, "If we get down 1–0 tonight, they will probably boo us out of the stadium. You have to do something great to get them out of their seats. Shoot, up in Cleveland, they were down three runs in the ninth inning and they were still on their feet."

Expectedly, the Atlanta–Fulton County Stadium crowd let him have it. While he stood on the on-deck circle in the first inning, a fan behind home plate lit into him, yelling "Justice, go to Philadelphia. Go anywhere. We don't want you here," the right fielder recalled to the *Chicago Tribune*.

He got partially back in their good graces with a double to left-center in the fourth inning. Then in the sixth, he heard them roar—and gave Glavine exactly what he was pleading for.

Just get me one.

Justice didn't have much of a history with Poole, seeing the left-handed reliever just once before, a Game Two meeting in which Poole fell behind 2–0 and 3–1 before Justice hit a deep fly ball to right field.

When the lefty came on with two outs in the fifth inning after Jones's two-out single—he beat out a slow roller to second base, tumbling over Murray's foot on first base as he did so—Justice watched from the on-deck circle.

McGriff was thrown three straight breaking balls, swinging and missing at the last two, and on the out pitch the massive first baseman lunged at the ball, landing awkwardly as he came up with nothing.

Justice strode to the plate to start the sixth with a clear plan after seeing McGriff's mistakes. "I was just thinking, 'I'm going to stay on the fastball,'" he said. "'I'm going to make him throw me a curveball for a strike before I even think about (swinging at it).'"

He watched Poole's first offering, a fastball on the outside half of the plate for strike one, then watched another miss high and away to even the count at 1–1. Justice started weighing Poole's options.

"The pivotal count was the 1–1, because usually 1–1 lefty to lefty, it might be a curveball coming now," he said. "But I was willing to take that curveball, because I wanted to see it as a strike, some kind of reference point."

Poole didn't make him have to sit on a curveball. He threw another fastball, this one up and in the middle. "That," Poole told the *Philadelphia Daily News*, "is a bad place to make a mistake."

Justice drove it into right field, a towering shot that Ramirez could only turn and watch as it sailed over the wall.

"It was a pitch that was supposed to be down and away, and it was up and in," Poole told the *Washington Post*.

Said Justice: "I stayed on the fastball and he gave me a fastball middle, in, and I was fortunate to get him."

He rounded first, punching at the air as the crowd roared behind him. "Dave Justice, all is forgiven in Atlanta," NBC play-by-play announcer Bob Costas said as Justice crossed the plate.

"They [the fans] proved me wrong," Justice told reporters after the game. "I was so happy to hear them screaming."

The rewards for that moment continued in the seventh inning as he was greeted with a standing ovation by the crowd and a walk on four pitches by reliever Alan Embree.

Justice had given Glavine his lead, but Glavine knew there was no room for error, especially with the heart of the Indians order coming up in the seventh inning.

"It was about a hitter at a time, an inning at a time, and nothing more than that," he said. "Because I knew how dangerous they were and how quickly things could change."

But he kept the Indians at bay once again as Baerga lined out to third, followed by a Belle strikeout. Murray walked on four pitches, but he would be the last baserunner Glavine would allow as he brought an end to the inning as Ramirez hit a deep out to left-center field.

When he went out to warm up for the eighth inning, Glavine knew he didn't have much left. "For whatever reason, things weren't as crisp," he said. "I didn't get loose as quickly as I had been up to that point in time."

It nearly cost him as Thome, who hit a 436-foot home run off Brad Clontz in the eighth inning of Game Five, nearly recreated that moment with Glavine. The third baseman jumped on the first pitch, a towering shot to left-center that Grissom hauled in two steps onto the warning track.

A Tony Pena popout to short right field and Ruben Amaro Jr.'s grounder to first, which McGriff flipped to Glavine, put the Braves three outs from a title.

As Glavine came off the field, he told Cox and Mazzone, "I'm mentally shot."

"Of course he's mentally shot, hell you don't think we know that?" Mazzone said. "He's trying to bring the first

championship in sports to Atlanta and when he was done
he was done."

He had thrown 109 pitches, 67 for strikes, with eight
strikeouts and three walks. Based on sabermetrics pioneer
Bill James's Game Score, which measures the strength of
a pitcher in a particular game, Glavine registered an 81.
It was the best performance in a World Series since Hershiser's 87 for the Dodgers in 1988 and was tied for the
thirteenth highest since World War II.

"He never gave in. He never made a mistake," Hart
said. "It was just a masterful pitching performance in a big
game against a really good offense, a great offense."

Of those previous one-hitters in World Series history,
only four had been parts of complete games, something no
one had done in twenty-eight years to that point.

The Braves nearly added to their lead to start the
eighth as Lopez battled reliever Julian Tavarez for 12
pitches. He smacked a 3–2 breaking ball and, sure he'd
hit it out, Lopez left the batter's box with both arms
extended—as if in flight. But Belle caught it just in
front of the left-field wall as a defeated Lopez was left
grimacing.

If there was any hope whether Glavine would come
out for the ninth, it was exorcised two batters after Lopez's
long out when Luis Polonia pinch-hit for him, a move that
drew boos from the Atlanta–Fulton County Stadium crowd
when it was announced.

Glavine admits now he was torn. As fitting as it might
have been that he put the Braves in position to claim that
elusive World Series title, he also wanted to be standing
there on the field when it happened.

"It was hard on a selfish note, because you have a
one-hit shutout going in the World Series," he said, "and
we all want to be that last guy on the mound when the season is over and you're champions, and to pitch a complete

game shutout in an environment like that would have been absolutely unbelievable."

But Thome's long out could have made his performance for naught, and after seeing the Braves lose in seven games to the Twins in 1991, Glavine wasn't about to press his luck.

"I know I got away with some stuff," he said.

It also helped having Mark Wohlers to lean on. He'd make his only All-Star Game appearance a year later when he saved 39 games. The big righty—he stood 6-foot-4, 207 pounds—converted 25 during the 1995 regular season.

Wohlers had blown a save in Game Three when he replaced Greg McMichael and gave up a run-scoring double to Sandy Alomar in a game the Indians would win 7–6 on Murray's walk-off single. Dating back to May 10, though, he had converted 30 of his 33 opportunities heading into Game Six, and Glavine was confident in the change of pace Wohlers presented with his 100-mph fastball.

"When you have a guy like Mark Wohlers, who was having the year that he was having, let him face those guys one time through the lineup throwing 95 opposed to me for the fourth time or fifth time, whatever it was," Glavine said.

Turned spectator, Glavine chewed on gum as he sat in the dugout, watching Wohlers go through his warmup pitches. With his slow leg kick and delivery, making his explosive arsenal seem almost out of place, Wohlers found himself behind Lofton 2–1. Lofton chopped at the fourth offering—a letter-high fastball—sending a blooper into foul territory in left field, one that Belliard, sprinting toward it from shortstop, hauled in with a back-handed grab.

"That's why the batting average doesn't matter so much," Costas said of Belliard, who hit .094 in the Series but had committed just one error in each of the past three seasons, a span of 212 games. "That's why Cox wants him in in the ninth."

The anticipation built as Wohlers pulled the Braves within one out of the title. Pinch-hitter Paul Sorrento, who had come off the bench to hit a double off the reliever in Game Four, warmed Grissom up for his defining catch, with a routine fly ball to center.

Owner Ted Turner, his wife Jane Fonda to his left—both wearing Braves hats—stood with his hands held together as if in prayer. To his right was a smiling Bill Murray, who wore a brown corduroy shirt and jeans. The actor was in Atlanta discussing a movie about former White Sox owner Bill Veeck, entitled *Veeck as in Wreck*, which Turner controlled the rights to.

Veeck was the forefather to Turner's old carnival barker ways, and the Atlanta owner was moments away from finding himself linked to Veeck in another way. The Hall of Famer Veeck would win only one title—in 1948, when he owned the very team Turner's Braves were finishing off, the Indians.

Mazzone, as was his trademark, rocked back and forth in one corner of the dugout, while outfielder Dwight Smith stood up and turned toward the crowd, waving a towel.

Wohlers adjusted his hat, blew out a deep breath, and gripped the ball in his glove as Baerga dug in. The closer raised his hands high above his head before slowly bringing them down in front of his face. He threw a waist-high fastball and Baerga's looping swing pushed the ball to the outfield as Grissom gave chase.

"I felt like I could retire from baseball at that moment," Grissom said of that title-clinching catch. "That's what I really felt like."

In the crowd, one fan held up the simplest of signs, one that seemed to sum up the previous four postseasons for these Braves. . . . "Finally!" the sign read in two-foot-tall letters.

After losing in seven games in '91 and four a year later, the Braves had their title. The hysteria that began with the players and coaches on the mound stretched across the field, Jones waving to the stands and blowing a kiss, with the tomahawk chop and war chant providing the soundtrack for it all.

In the clubhouse the Braves pulled on their championship T-shirts and hats, Bill Bartholomay, Stan Kasten, and John Schuerholz joining Turner and Cox on stage as they held the World Series trophy.

"Of all the things I hadn't accomplished, this was the one thing I really wanted," Turner said.

Glavine sprayed a bottle of rose-colored champagne before he was awarded the MVP trophy after going 2–0 with a 1.29 ERA and 11 strikeouts to six walks. He was the sixth starting pitcher to take the honor in the last eight World Series.

"I think it's just that, for us it was so many things," Glavine said. "Obviously, the battle to get there, knowing what it means to be World Series champions and all that and the work you put in.

"But I think for that group of guys, even more than that, it was the frustrations that we had before that, losing in '91 and '92, getting beat in the NLCS in '93, the strike in '94, so there was a lot of frustration that led to that and to ultimately be able to experience that with a lot of the same guys, a lot of those core guys that went through those frustrations, I think that made it much more special."

For both the players and a city whose residents came out in droves. An estimated 500,000 strong showed up for the 2.2-mile-long championship parade that went down Peachtree Street, going past City Hall and ending at Atlanta–Fulton County Stadium.

Turner and Fonda rode atop the lead fire truck with Schuerholz, the World Series trophy beside them. The entire team rode atop trucks, a move that came in response to 1991, when over 750,000 came out—it was the largest gathering in Atlanta history—and players who rode in open cars were overwhelmed by a crowd that stood fifteen deep in some places.

"Hopefully this winter," Glavine would say, "we can keep everybody on this team . . . hint, hint."

He was largely talking about McGriff. In all McGriff hit 27 homers and 27 doubles with 93 RBIs and a .280/.361/.489 slash line and filed for free agency in November. But the first baseman re-signed for $20 million over four years.

"Who wouldn't want to play for a team that just won it all?" McGriff told the *Atlanta Journal-Constitution.*

Tom Glavine allowed one hit over eight innings in Game Six–marking the fifth one-hitter in World Series history–to clinch the Braves' title. (*jimmyack205*)

With McGriff wrapped up, the core of Glavine, Maddux, and Smoltz as the anchor, and a payroll that sat at $53 million—the highest in the NL and trailing only the Yankees ($61.5 million) and Orioles ($55.1 million) overall—the Braves were in position to follow their title with another.

In 1996, Atlanta won 96 games, claiming an MLB-best 56 at home. It had another Cy Young recipient in Smoltz, who was 24–8 with a 2.94 ERA and 276 strikeouts.

The Braves steamrolled through the Dodgers, winning the division series in three games before beating the Cardinals in seven to make a return to the World Series to take on the Yankees.

Claiming the first two games by a combined 16–1 and pounding out 23 hits to New York's seven, Atlanta was halfway toward another coronation.

Glavine exited Game Three, having allowed one run on four hits in seven innings, but reliever Greg McMichael gave up a two-run blast to Bernie Williams that put the game out of reach as the Braves fell 5–2.

Atlanta bounced back the following night, racing out to a 6–0 lead behind a four-run fourth that included a solo homer by McGriff and a two-run double via Grissom.

Then came the second biggest comeback in World Series history.

Their lead cut in half in the sixth, Cox opted to go to Wohlers to record the final six outs. But after giving up singles to Charlie Hayes and Darryl Strawberry to start the eighth, Jim Leyritz came off the bench to hit a game-tying home run.

The Yankees would win in 10 behind a bases-loaded pinch-hit walk by Wade Boggs and Hayes reaching on a Klesko error to score Jeter.

Only the 1929 Philadelphia Athletics, who scored 10 runs in the seventh to beat the Cubs 10–8 in Game Four, had mounted a bigger rally on the game's grandest stage.

It proved a turning point as the Yankees won 1–0 and 3–2 in the next two games to capture the title.

"I know I can't let '96 go," Smoltz said. "[That] personally for me, was one of the best years I ever had. It was almost a dream year for the team and to come up short like we did, that was a game-changer."

The Yankees would go on to claim three more titles with that same core, winning from 1998 to 2000, and while the Braves made the NLCS the next two years, their season ended there. They did return to the World Series in 1999, falling to the Yankees again, but did so with a very different roster.

Atlanta went through a roster overhaul, as Avery left to join the Red Sox as a free agent in January 1997, and two months later, Justice and Grissom were shipped to Cleveland for Lofton.

McGriff was sold to the Devil Rays in November 1997, and that same month, Lemke (Red Sox) and Blauser (Cubs) left via free agency. By the time the Braves and Yankees met for another title, just five Atlanta position players (Andruw Jones, Chipper Jones, Klesko, Lopez, and Eddie Perez) and four pitchers (Glavine, Maddux, Smoltz, and Wohlers) remained from '95.

"That shifted our organization and shifted another [the Yankees] in a direction where we could have done what they did," Smoltz said. "No doubt in my mind, we win that World Series our team doesn't change that much and we're looking at four out of five and who knows what happens?"

The core of that Braves team produced three Hall of Famers in Glavine, Maddux, and Smoltz, and put Cox in Cooperstown, with Chipper Jones expected to follow when he's eligible in 2018 and Schuerholz at some point, too.

That they won only one championship while claiming a record 14 consecutive division titles is the only knock against their dominance.

"I've got to say this: fourteen in a row and every year having a chance to do it, coming so close to winning four or five championships still eats at me," Smoltz said. "It really does."

For Glavine, whose defining game came in giving the Braves that lone title, the feelings of that night are unforgettable, far outreaching the frustrations of '91, '92, and '99.

"Those are things that I think will stay with me for the rest of my life," he said.

"We appreciated winning every year, even though we only got one ring," Maddux said. "We enjoyed the individual success, the team success, we enjoyed all that while we were going through it. I don't think we strayed too far from our next start, though. Which was probably one of the reasons we had so much success. We were pretty good about just trying to win today."

* * * *

Faye and Melvin Perry would reconnect in Virginia, mother and son spending the holidays together with the rest of their family. She had put her parents in charge of raising Melvin—who would move him to Virginia and, later, Connecticut—and when they saw each other for Thanksgiving in 1995, Faye came with something in hand.

A baseball.

The game was something they could share. Melvin grew up a Mets fan, and when his mom was hired by the Braves "it was great because we got to talk baseball," he said. They would razz each other when Atlanta and New

York faced off, and when the Braves made the '95 World Series Melvin told her good luck, but "I'm not rooting for you necessarily."

"I've got something for you," Faye told her then-29-year-old son.

"What?" he asked.

"Well, you know Marquis caught the last out?"

"Yeah."

"Well, this is the ball."

"Oh, wow," Melvin replied. "He doesn't want it?"

"He gave it to me," the mother said. "And I'm giving it to you."

"Mom, you don't have to do that. That's yours."

"No," she insisted. "I want to give it to you."

For the last twenty years, the ball has been with Melvin. He's been married and divorced and the ball has moved with him.

"It's safe," Melvin said. "It's always been safe."

A number of balls from the final out of World Series are on public display, with those from 1903, 1962, 1968, and 2004 among the ones in the Hall of Fame. The latter came with controversy as Doug Mientkiewicz unwittingly became in possession of the ball from the Red Sox' first title in eighty-six years and, expecting it to be returned after lending it to the team, donated it in '06 after his wife's life was threatened.

Some players have kept the final-out ball, while others have given it away, including the Yankees' Chad Curtis, who in a story similar to Faye Perry's, signed the ball before giving it to a Yankee Stadium security guard in 1999.

But it's the 2000 ball that may share the closest relationship to the '95 edition.

That ball belongs to Bernie Williams, the Yankees center fielder and, in retirement, a Grammy-nominated jazz musician. Williams is a classically trained guitarist and Melvin Perry shares that world as the vocalist and bass player for the three-member funk band Solistic.

Based out of Fairfield County, Connecticut, the group has released four albums.

"The entire artistic package, that's what we're about," Perry said. "That's kind of what our music is about. I write the lyrics; I'm the singer. I pay as much attention to lyrical content as it is to the music and I want our whole artistic package to be something people can listen to over and over again."

In 2010, it was estimated the final out from the Phillies' 1980 win would fetch six-figures, but Perry's ball marks the one and only championship for the city of Atlanta. It's a valuable piece of the game's past—that being said, owning the ball isn't something he tries to overanalyze.

"The fact that I have this baseball, yeah, being a fan of history I understand the historical aspect but it's not overpowering to me," he said. "I'm honored to have this ball that Marquis gave to my mother and my mother gave to me.

"But in the scope of things, it's a baseball."

One baseball that—in going from a center fielder to a security guard, and ultimately her bass-playing son—has gone on the oddest of journeys.

Chapter Ten

Bobby Cox: The Players' Manager

Everyone has a Bobby Cox story. It's just that Tom Glavine's may be the most telling tale of what the Braves' Hall of Fame manager stood for during his decades in the game.

The left-hander was sitting in the dugout, where nearby Cox was going over his lineup card while the Braves were out on the field, weighing over whom he was going to bring out of the bullpen. His glasses—as they often were—were perched down on his nose.

"He wasn't even watching the game," Glavine recalls. "Didn't even see the pitch that was thrown."

No matter. Someone on the bench shouted that it should have been called a strike and that was enough for Cox. He jumped out of his seat, trotted out onto the field, and lit into the umpire.

"But that's just how he was," said Glavine, who spent seventeen years with Cox as his manager. "'What? Somebody was . . . Okay, I'm on it.' It was so special for his players, knowing he was going to fight tooth-and-nail for every inch for his players and his team."

In twenty-five years with the Braves, and another four in Toronto, the manager would claim fifteen division titles, five pennants, and a World Series ring, and had won the fourth-most games in history upon his retirement in 2010. His legacy, though, doesn't reside in those banners. It doesn't reside in trophies, nor with his place on the all-time wins list.

Cox's career is best measured in the loyalty that his player-friendly ways inspired from those who suited up for him—and of course, those record ejections. He was tossed 158 times in the regular season and another three in the playoffs.

But it's those elements that fed the two pillars of Bobby Cox's success: passion and compassion.

"There's no other reason to go anywhere else when you have a manager that you can trust and love and want to play for," said John Smoltz, who played twenty of his twenty-one MLB seasons for Cox.

The compassion came through in the little things. It was in the way he greeted his players when they came to the ballpark, cutting through their profession and finding out about who these people were.

Marquis Grissom had played for three different managers during his six seasons with the Expos—Buck Rodgers, Tom Runnells, and Felipe Alou—and when he arrived in Atlanta in 1995, he found something different in Cox.

"He's the best, from all the managers I had, and just experiencing all the managers that I had," Grissom said. "Every day he would ask me 'How you doing? How's your family doing?'

Bobby Cox's 2,405 career wins included a franchise-best 2,149 with the Braves. (*SD Kirk*)

"(He was) able to push all of us in the right direction and get the best out of all of us, and I think that says the world about Bobby Cox—and if you can't play for him, you can't play for nobody."

That's what John Schuerholz, Atlanta's general manager for seventeen seasons of Cox's run, calls his "great human characteristic."

"He values you enough to learn enough about you and your family and your background, so you start out on a human level of another human being caring enough about you that he wants to learn about you," Schuerholz said. "He wants to know who you are. He wants to have sensitivity about what's going on in your life. He will do that.

"Not many people who are as good as what he was and is and excellent, not good, excellent at what he did in his profession. Not many people have to do that. Bobby did it because it's in his heart. It's who he is as a human."

Said Fredi Gonzalez, Cox's successor in the Braves dugout, "He's a genuine guy. That's something you watch. He'd rather spend an hour with the groundskeepers than sit in a room with all the media guys and that kind of stuff.

"He could have dinner with the president of the United States in the White House one weekend and then he'd be having lunch with the groundskeepers back here or the guys digging ditches on the side of the road and [they'd] get the same guy."

That ability to break down walls and connect to individuals played itself out on the field, as his charges never doubted his belief in them.

It was the story of John Smoltz's career. Cox's refusal to remove him from the rotation in 1991 while he was 2–11 helped pave the way for a Hall of Fame career.

"The confidence that Bobby exudes in people when nobody else has it," Smoltz says is his best attribute. "Every player goes through a slump. Every player loses confidence, and when your manager somehow instills that in you, you look at him and you're like 'Are you crazy?' and it helps you get through it."

If the man who dictates their playing time has total faith in them, why would his players think or act any differently?

"It's hard to go out on the field where you're kind of doubting whether your manager thinks you can come through in certain situations," said Mark Lemke, the

Braves second baseman from 1988 to 1997. "But we always had the backing of Bobby Cox. He always backed all his players."

In January 2002, Brian Jordan was hitting in the Turner Field batting cage, laughing and joking with his manager. But as he pulled out of the ballpark and drove home a call came. It was Schuerholz.

"Hey, Brian," Schuerholz said. "We made a trade today."

"John, who did we get?" the right fielder replied.

"Well," Schuerholz replied, "We picked up Gary Sheffield from the Dodgers."

Jordan's thoughts immediately went to an outfield consisting of himself, Sheffield, who was a six-time All-Star, and Andruw Jones, the winner of four straight Gold Gloves in center field.

"I'm sitting there like 'Holy nuts!'" Jordan said. "Oh, we're going to win the championship this year. I'm pumped and said 'Who did we have to give up?'"

"We had to give up Odalis Perez and some minor leaguers," Schuerholz answered.

Jordan couldn't believe it. The Braves were fleecing the Dodgers, but then there was a long pause on the GM's end.

"I thought 'Hell, no,'" Jordan said. "Is he going to tell me I got traded?"

"The only way the deal could go down, [is] the Dodgers wanted you," Schuerholz said.

"John," Jordan said, "I think I better hang up the phone now before I say something I regret."

He ended the call, his world turned on its head. When he signed with Atlanta as a free agent, Cox was a major draw for the Virginia native.

"It was tough, because I loved Atlanta—that was home for me—I loved playing for Bobby Cox," Jordan said. "To me my world was perfect and then to be traded away, God, that was like a bomb going off."

But then Cox called him.

"Brian, I'm so sorry," he said. "Your name was never mentioned in any trades. I'm still in disbelief. I would have told you. I would have called you into the office down at the stadium if I would have known, but your name was never mentioned in any trade. I'm really mad right now."

Three years later, in 2005, Jordan was a free agent again, and he came back to Atlanta to play the final two seasons of his career for Cox.

"I got the call and the opportunity to come back and I was like 'I'm there,'" he said.

Years ago, Cox told pitching coach Leo Mazzone, "It didn't do me any good when I was playing, somebody screaming at me all the time. Now, there's a place for it. There's a place to be firm every once in a while."

When he needed to be firm, he did so privately. He didn't take gripes public, nor scoldings, but more often than not, he didn't even have to verbalize any issues with players.

"Bobby did it in a quiet fashion," said his former third baseman and hitting coach, Terry Pendleton. "Sometimes he didn't have to say anything to you, it was a look he gave you. It was a reaction that he gave you."

The way he handled people fueled the entire vibe around the team.

"He made it a joy to come to the ballpark, whether we won the game before or we lost the game before," Mazzone said. "We couldn't wait to get to the ballpark to be around him, because he had that aura about him as far as just a great person. You can't find that anywhere else.

"I've never found it in anybody else in my lifetime, being in the game for forty-two years. I haven't found anybody that could come close to matching the makeup of Bobby Cox."

Gonzalez, who was Cox's third-base coach for three years, didn't ask him many questions when they were together and didn't hound him.

"I just watched, watched and learned," Gonzalez said. "Sure, every once in a while, 'Skip, what was this?' But if you watched and paid attention, the way he handled himself and handled people around him, you would pick up a lot of stuff."

But when Gonzalez is dealing with a difficult decision or wondering how to handle a situation, he picks up the phone for his Hall of Fame sounding board.

"It's priceless to be able to pick up the phone and ask him those questions," Gonzalez said. "Those types of words of wisdom or words of advice, to this day."

Down the dugout steps toward the tunnel to the clubhouse in Turner Field sits a small room with multiple televisions and a couple of chairs.

"That was the Ejection Room," Jordan said. "That's what I would call it, because Bobby would just hang out there and he would always communicate back and forth, guys would always walk down there and he's sitting right there.

"You knew what to do the rest of the game; coaches knew what to do."

Ejections. They're unavoidable when the topic turns to Cox, whose record is 29 more than second-place John McGraw and nearly double that of Tony La Russa, who joined him in the 2014 Hall of Fame class.

Cox climbed atop the all-time list on August 15, 2007, tossed by home-plate umpire Ted Barrett for arguing a called third strike on Chipper Jones to end the fifth inning against the Giants.

"It's nothing," Cox would say afterward. "It just means I've been around a long time."

After Barrett's third-strike call, Jones threw his bat, and then his helmet. "[Barrett] and I didn't see eye-to-eye on the strike zone, and Bobby knows if I'm that upset, that's a ball," Jones told reporters.

The third baseman started walking toward his position and, meanwhile, Cox was laying into the umpire. He would be ousted for the fifty-third time in his career for arguing balls and strikes.

"I think when Bobby saw that I wasn't long for this game, he took over," Jones said.

But like so many of his ejections, the record, fittingly, came while Cox was protecting a player.

"Now, I didn't particularly like being on deck when he got ejected or he was yelling at the umpires," Jordan said. "He did it constantly. He protected his pitchers and he was into every pitch of the game.

"I tell you what, he protected those pitchers. He would argue balls and strikes all game long."

Jordan recalls being on deck when Cox was giving the umpire an earful. He turned to his manager and said, "Could you be quiet? I've got to go up there next. I don't want the umpires getting mad at me."

In July 2006 in San Diego, Jeff Francoeur struck out in the seventh inning and said something to home-plate umpire Bruce Dreckman that he took exception to, giving Francoeur his first career ejection. But then Cox trotted out, giving Dreckman an earful. He was tossed too.

As they made their way to the visiting clubhouse, Francoeur asked him, "What do I do? I've never been thrown out of a game."

"Ah, go up, have a few beers, relax," Cox said. "You're going to get fined $500, or you can do what I do and send in a $10,000 check and tell them 'Call me when I owe more.'"

Looking back, Francoeur says of that moment "I love it, because that was him. When you went out there to argue and got tossed, he was coming with you. That meant the world to me."

Said pitcher Tim Hudson, who was with Cox from 2005 to 2010: "Those kinds of managers, the players in those locker rooms would fight hell backward for them.

"Bobby was one of the best. He was one of the best at letting his guys know 'You know what? I'm going to put it on the line for you and I expect you to do the same for me.' He was awesome at that."

Cox's old-school ways included his attire. He wore metal cleats. Every game.

"I've never seen a manager wear cleats before," former Brave Eric Hinske told SI.com in 2010. "And he's fully uni'd up always when we get here. He puts his cleats on right away—sanitaries and old-school stirrups too."

Pitcher Paul Byrd once asked Cox about his footwear of choice. Why, while other managers wore turf shoes or running shoes, was he still in cleats?

"Paul," Cox replied, "you never know when they might need me."

"I loved that," Byrd said.

Cox set the tone in the Braves' clubhouse upon his arrival for his first stint as manager in 1978. Every year at spring training he would lay out a list of six rules.

1. No beards
2. No uniform pants covering the shoe tops
3. Dress code
4. Mind the curfew

5. Be on time

6. Play hard at all times

"You knew what you had in Bobby Cox," Jordan said. "All that he wanted from you was to play hard and be on time. Those were his big rules. . . . For me, that was easy, and I knew I was going to play hard anyway."

Andruw Jones learned just how deep those rules ran in a July game in 1998, when he didn't run all-out at a ball hit to center. Cox pulled him off the field in the middle of the game, then months later was comparing him to Willie Mays and calling him the greatest he'd ever seen at the position.

Jones had earned a little retribution days after being yanked as he, after striking out on a wild pitch against the Phillies, tore off down the line to reach safely. He would score three batters later in a 3–2 win.

"I heard the ball hit the ground and I said 'Okay, I've got to run,'" Jones said after the game. "I just hustled to first."

Once viewed as brandishing a smirk that underscored the fact that he didn't care, here was Jones talking about hustle just days after being booed for a lack of it?

Consider it a by-product of Cox's rules, which came from his days with the Yankees—for whom he played a combined 220 games in 1968 and 1969 and began his managerial career in their farm system in 1971. The majority of his expectations boiled down to projecting an appearance, whether on the field or off.

"He taught me to not only be dressed good [at the ballpark], [but] dress good outside, dress good at the hotel, going to a restaurant, going to the ballpark," said catcher Eddie Perez. "He said 'We've got to dress nice. There's people around. We have to look like a professional player.'"

Over the years, Cox would bend on the beard rule, and he'd allow the bottom of the pants to go a little bit lower. But he always decided how the clubhouse would operate: what would be tolerated and what wouldn't.

"It was set by Bobby, because that's the manager's domain," Schuerholz said. "Clubhouse is the manager's domain, not the general manager's domain. Some general managers try to make it theirs and they don't last long. Ultimately they don't last long. Ultimately it's not their domain."

If a new player arrived and didn't live up to the expectations Cox had set in place, the veterans would take it upon themselves to set them straight.

"If anybody broke a rule, we'd tell them 'Hey, you're doing this wrong. Bobby doesn't like that.'" Perez said. "As soon as you say that, he will change everything. You won't go to somebody and say 'the Braves don't do that here,' but as soon as you say 'Bobby doesn't like that,' everything changed."

Dale Murphy played for two Hall of Fame managers, Cox and Joe Torre. Both had the ability to get players to feel something that went deeper than the typical professional athlete/manager relationship.

"There's a point in time when you're actually playing for them," Murphy said. "NFL, NBA, any professional sport at the highest level, a coach or manager needs to figure out how to create the same feeling that you have for your high school coach or your college coach, that you're actually playing for the leader of the team."

Mazzone saw it in the ways players hated to lose, not only for the mere fact of losing a game, but because they didn't want to disappoint Bobby.

"I had Glavine or Maddux or Smoltz come to me many times and go 'Man, I hate it that we lose that game, but I hate it more for Bobby than anything else,'" he said.

"You heard that a lot and they heard it from me, they heard it from the coaches, and that's how everybody felt."

Said Glavine, "I've always said that when I had a bad game I felt awful because I felt like I let him down more than I let myself down. To have somebody mean that much to you is pretty rare, but to have that somebody mean that much to so many guys that played for him is unbelievable."

Change the context and it sounds as though they're talking about a father or a grandfather. To many, that was what Cox represented. He took on that role for generations that watched him from afar on the bench, and to those who played for him.

"I've always said he is the second greatest figure in my life behind my dad," Glavine said. "There are times when you were playing for him that you felt like you were playing for your dad."

Glavine began playing for Cox as a 24-year-old, but the manager had that same effect on veterans like Pendleton.

Pendleton showed up in Atlanta in 1991 as a 30-year-old and would play for Cox in two different stints ('91–'94 and '96). He stuck around afterward, becoming the Braves' hitting coach from 2002 to 2010.

"You wanted to please him," Pendleton said. "You wanted to go out every day and please him in the way you went about playing the game, that your actions on and off the field were very important and you wanted to make sure you were upholding what he stood for, whether he said it or not, you knew what he stood for."

Perez was another of Cox's former players who stayed on after their careers. A catcher from 1995 to 1999 and again in 2004 and 2005 after stops in Cleveland and Milwaukee, Cox brought Perez on in 2007 as the bullpen coach.

To Perez, Cox was much more than just a manager.

"I look at Bobby as my mentor, my friend, the one that taught me everything in the big leagues," Perez said. "Everybody was trying because they knew he cared about everybody, that's something that I wish people knew about Bobby Cox, the way he was, the way he treated you, the way he talked to you, the way he cares about you.

"It's probably something people missed because he was a great manager and he won a lot of games and all you want to do when you step onto the field was give him 100 percent."

One of Cox's first moves when he took over as Braves manager in June 1990—for the second time—was to bring on Mazzone as his pitching coach.

Mazzone was the guru who helped elevate all-time talents like the Big Three of Glavine, Smoltz, and Greg Maddux along with Steve Avery and on and on. But he stresses that Cox played just as big of a hand in the effectiveness of Braves pitching.

"He's the greatest handler of pitchers in the history of the game," Mazzone said. "I think Bobby's in the Hall of Fame because of the way he treated people and his knowledge of pitching and how to handle pitchers. I didn't run into too many managers in my career that understood that part of the game."

At a visit to the Hall of Fame, Cox was visiting with Sandy Koufax and Tom Seaver—both HOFers for their exploits on the mound—and he told Schuerholz after their talk that it was eye opening. "I thought I knew a lot about pitching," Cox said.

"Bobby always recognized from a very young age as a player, and then as a young minor-league manager, then as a major-league manager, how important pitching is," Schuerholz said. "He learned it and he studied it and he asked questions about it and he's still asking questions about it."

The Cox/Mazzone partnership would last for fifteen-plus seasons, the two being fixtures as much as the legendary arms that topped their rotations, and the pitching coach is unabashed in his feelings toward the man he owes it all to.

"He gave me my opportunity to go to the big leagues and it meant everything in the world to me," Mazzone said. "My dad just passed away here recently, and Bobby Cox had the most influence on me in my lifetime with the exception of my father as far as male . . . he had a tremendous influence on my career, because I wouldn't have had a career without him."

And there may have been no Braves reign in the 1990s and 2000s had it not been for Cox's second act in Atlanta.

In October 1981, Braves owner Ted Turner gave Cox a chance to state his case to save his job. The team had gone 50–56 in the strike-shortened season, which dropped Cox to 266–323.

Four years earlier, Turner had hired Cox away from the world champion Yankees, saying, "We're hoping Bobby can be the manager to lead us to the promised land as soon as possible."

He was picked over the likes of former Yankee and Mets manager Yogi Berra, because, as Turner said, "We have a young team and wanted someone who was young and had his future ahead instead of behind him."

At 36, Cox was the youngest manager in the NL and two years the junior of Atlanta pitcher Phil Niekro. But coming off a 101-loss season, Turner was feeling pressure after predicting a World Series in five years when he bought the team in 1976.

That fifth season—1980—would see the Braves go 81–80. It was progress after dropping 93 games in Cox's first season and 94 the second, but in 1981 Atlanta was 43–42 on September 12, and would then drop 14 of their final 21 games.

"Obviously, this goes back to the last three weeks, when we pulled a choke," Turner said. "But you can't necessarily blame it on the manager. The players are the ones who choked. But then, the manager is supposed to keep them calmed down. That's part of his job, isn't it? But that's not to say he can always do that."

The irony here is that just over a year before this, Turner said—after months of speculation that Cox would be fired— "Tell him not to worry about the rumors. Tell him he's got a job next season and for as long as he wants it."

But two days after his trial by Ted, Cox was done, telling the manager of his decision in a private meeting at Turner's CNN office. Cox was offered a scouting position, but refused with the intent he'd be back in a dugout the following season.

"Ted just told me a change was needed and we didn't have a great year," Cox would say. "We didn't have a terrible year either. . . . I think the team has come leaps and bounds. The Braves were little more than an expansion club when I got here."

Turner told reporters at the time he'd leaned on his front office staff, which included general manager John Mullen, Hank Aaron (director of player development), Paul Snyder (director of scouting), and Pat Nugent (assistant GM), and who recommended the dismissal.

But Mullen would tell writers that at the team's end-of-the-season meeting, Cox's future never came up until Turner called that group back for a second meeting.

Cox's "expansion team" comment took on a bit of irony a week later when he was named manager of the Blue Jays, a team that had been in existence for five years.

He had also been in discussions with the Mets, who had fired Joe Torre.

"There was some interest from some of the other clubs that had fired their managers but nothing specific," Cox told reporters. "But there were a number of reasons why I chose Toronto over New York."

He mentioned the team's commitment to him, its farm system, and young right-hander Dave Stieb. But, really, Cox said, "Deep down my heart I wanted to be here."

Cox appeared at that 1981 press conference for his firing, and Turner expressed his affection for his former manager, saying he "has been and will continue to be a close personal friend."

Nevertheless, the team would move forward with Torre, a 41-year-old former Braves player (1966–1969), despite the front office's recommendation of Triple-A Richmond manager Eddie Haas. Niekro had also been interested in a player/manager role.

"We considered Haas and Niekro, but I really felt like we needed someone with major-league experience," Turner said. "I wanted someone not real old that had experience and didn't have a drinking problem or whatever."

Torre seemed a deft move, as he led the Braves to a division title in 1982 behind Murphy's bat, but he was ousted after three years in which he never finished lower than second in the division.

Turner's rationale? Torre said, "Ted felt he wanted to make a change at this time. He wanted to go in a different direction. I never asked for another reason."

This time, Turner listened to his confidants, hiring Haas in 1985. But Haas was gone after 121 games and replaced by Bobby Wine, amid a season in which Atlanta dropped 96 games and finished fifth in the West.

Meanwhile, Cox was building something in Toronto.

After going 78–84 in his debut to come in sixth out of seven teams in the East, he then rattled off three straight winning seasons as the Blue Jays climbed to fourth and second before winning the division at 99–62 in 1985. They finished one game out of the World Series, falling to the Royals in seven games in the American League Championship Series.

Cox would be named AL Manager of the Year by the Baseball Writers Association of America after that '85 run, only he was no longer leading the Jays when word came down.

Two weeks before that announcement, Turner came calling with a chance to come home.

Cox's family stayed in Marietta, Georgia, when he moved to Canada, and when Turner offered him the role of general manager, the 44-year-old took the opportunity to rejoin them full-time.

"I don't care how much money I'm being paid, I would never have left Toronto if it weren't for my family," he told United Press International in the spring of '86. "I had to think of my family for the first time in my life. I'm not getting any younger and this business is hard on a family."

Seeking a proven winner, the Braves teamed Cox with manager Chuck Tanner, who had led the Pirates to a championship in 1979. But he couldn't dig the Braves out of the West cellar, dropping 89 and 92 games his first two seasons before he was axed 39 games into 1989.

During Tanner's first season, *Pittsburgh Post Gazette* writer Charley Feeney wrote "he had a five-year contract, but his boss, Ted Turner, has been known to do strange things. If America's Team goes sour, Turner might suggest that Tanner and general manager Bobby Cox switch jobs for one month, one season or whatever."

He wasn't far off.

Tanner's replacement, Russ Nixon, did no better, going 130–216, and 65 games into 1990, he was out.

"I called Russ this morning and told him it was not a good phone call," Cox said at the time. "He knew what I meant."

He'd be replaced by the man who gave him that bad news. Cox moved back into the position he vacated nearly nine years before. But he'd do so with a talent pool that was far richer than the last time.

Cox's moves helped make up much of the core of the 1990s title teams and included two of the greatest players in franchise history. He traded aging Doyle Alexander for Smoltz in 1987 and drafted Avery and Chipper Jones in the first rounds in 1988 and 1990, respectively.

"When I got there, we made a decision to develop a strong farm system," Cox said. "All of our budget went into scouting, and there was little for the big club.

"We spent a lot of money on that plan. A plan can be a great plan and fail. Fortunately, our plan worked."

Cox's drafts also included the likes of Kent Mercker in '86; an '87 haul with Brian Hunter, Keith Mitchell, and Mike Stanton; in '88 he took Mark Wohlers; and in '89 he grabbed Ryan Klesko.

"What Bobby Cox and the great scouting system that we had here in the eighties did to get all these kids, that was the huge piece," Pendleton said, "because I can say this: every year that I was here, if somebody went down, we had a kid in the minor leagues ready to replace him and ready to go.

"That says something special about the scouts, the managers, the coaching staff, the directors down in the minors. That spoke volumes about Bobby when he was general manager and running things."

He did send out future Cy Young winner Steve Bedrosian in 1985, and made the unpopular move of sending Murphy to the Phillies on August 4, 1990, for Jeff Parrett,

Jim Vatcher, and Victor Rosario. But the latter move opened the door for David Justice.

He also dealt for Charlie Leibrandt and Francisco Cabrera, got Lonnie Smith off the scrap heap, purchased Vinny Castilla and Jeff Treadway, and signed the likes of Perez, Javy Lopez, and Greg Olson.

"He's everything," Smoltz said. "I mean I can't think of one person that has affected a career more than me. Than one player in the big leagues.

"You're talking about a GM that trades for you, a GM that trades for you that becomes your manager your whole career, a manager that sticks with you when you're 2–11 and everyone else wanted you out of the rotation and then of course, the reason—and sole reason—that I played all that time for Atlanta."

The lives touched are almost innumerable and his career achievements beyond reproach, that move back to the bench launching one of the greatest runs in American sports history. From 1991's Worst-to-First season through the Baby Braves and the '05 division title, Cox would win 1,431 games. That's 65 more than any other team in that period.

But Bobby Cox was always humble—that is, until an umpire would strike the match to light that fuse.

"He's a great man, a great man . . . and obviously, a great manager," Schuerholz said.

In 2010, his decades-long career ended, and like so many other final seasons for legends, it included a farewell tour.

"Being able to understand and see everybody in baseball, every team, every player just appreciating what he brought to the game of baseball and to see how everybody was just sending him off was something special to see from the same dugout as him," Hudson said. "It was awesome."

City after city meant gifts and ceremonies, a celebration of his impact, and one of those tributes included what could have been a rather humbling moment.

While in Washington, DC, in May to play the Nationals, Cox was invited to a reception on Capitol Hill hosted by senators Johnny Isakson of Georgia and West Virginia's Jay Rockefeller. The fete included a birthday cake for the manager, whose decorative writing read THANKS FOR 50 GREAT YEARS BOBBY COCKS.

A spokesperson for Isakson said the unfortunate phallic misspelling was the work of a local catering company, who never specified to the baker they were using how to spell the manager's last name.

Cox, though, didn't see it. He said the cake was already cut when he was given a piece. But when told of the error, the man who once said that those who consider him the most influential person in Braves history "need to get their head examined," simply laughed it off.

"That's funny," he told the *Atlanta Journal-Constitution.* "What bakery did he get that cake [from]? That's what I want to know."

Chapter Eleven

The Magic of Mazzone and McDowell

He was a gum-chomping, rocking, human perpetual-motion machine, the lasting image him sitting on the bench moving back and forth.

"Rocking is something I did when I was a kid," Leo Mazzone said. "I did it my whole life and didn't even know I was doing it."

He's blunt, he's opinionated, and has an outsized personality, and if it seems built for talk radio, well, he's done that too.

Mazzone's successor is reserved, calculated even. It's a departure for a reliever who, during his twelve-year major-league career, was known for putting his uniform on upside down—pants on top, jersey on bottom, with his shoes on his hands—setting off fireworks in the dugout bat rack, or wearing masks and wigs. But the role has helped to reshape him.

"I've got responsibility to these guys," Roger McDowell said. "There's more substance than just the guy that screws around."

The two couldn't be more different.

It's in their natures, their statures, approaches and their paths to becoming the Braves pitching coach. But their successes? Those have made them among the best in the modern era.

From 1991 to 2005, Mazzone's staffs had a collective 3.53 ERA, the best in the majors. They would produce nine 20-game winners, six Cy Young Awards, nine single-season team ERA titles, and three Hall of Famers in Tom Glavine, Greg Maddux, and John Smoltz.

McDowell, who had Smoltz during his last three seasons in Atlanta, has produced the second-lowest ERA in the majors at 3.78 since taking over for Mazzone in 2006. The Braves trail only the Dodgers and three-time Cy Young winner Clayton Kershaw's 3.67 in that span.

"I think Roger is the right guy for this era," said Atlanta bullpen coach and former catcher Eddie Perez. "I don't think Leo would work with those guys right now. It's different now. . . . I think Roger is perfect for being here and working with those guys and having that program and it's different because of the time. For then, Leo was perfect."

After arriving in Las Vegas in 1996's *Swingers*, Vince Vaughn's Trent grabs an unsuspecting cocktail waitress and points her gaze in the direction of his friend, Mikey (Jon Favreau). "I want you to remember this face, here. Okay?" he says, using a line that originated in the 1988 film *Things Change*. "This is the guy behind the guy behind the guy."

For the last twenty-five years, the guy behind the guy behind the guy for the Braves—a franchise whose reputation has largely been built on their pupils—has been Mazzone or McDowell.

While Bobby Cox's Atlanta coaching tree includes five former players or staff members who have gone on to become major-league managers—Don Baylor, Fredi Gonzalez, Walt Weiss, Jimy Williams, and Ned Yost—it's that duo of pitching coaches that will likely go down as his greatest hires.

Braves president and former general manager John Schuerholz says both "have instincts." To him, it's "but a combination of knowledge/intelligence of a subject and great experience in that subject, in that profession."

From that end, he points to that as what has fueled the accomplishments of both coaches.

"They came about it from different pathways," Schuerholz said, "but they're both very good."

*   *   *   *

It was late June 1990, and the Triple-A Richmond Braves had just returned to their Buffalo hotel when a call came for Leo Mazzone.

"I want you to make another trip," the voice on the other end said as Mazzone picked up the phone.

He had recently been to Seattle for a scouting trip for Bobby Cox, the major-league team's general manager, where he was asked to give his assessment of the Mariners' Michael Jackson, whom the Braves were considering landing with a package of Kent Mercker and Mike Stanton. Mazzone had found out Jackson's elbow was bothering him, a report that ended Atlanta's interest.

So when Cox called that night, he was certain he would once again be looking at an arm the Braves were interested in acquiring.

"Where do you want me to go now?" he asked.

"Can you be in Atlanta tomorrow at noontime?" Cox replied.

"Well, yeah," Mazzone said. "What's going on?"

"Well, Leo," Cox told him. "It's time. . . . We're naming you the pitching coach. Now, don't go crazy. I know how emotional you are. Is there anybody in the lobby?"

"Well, we just got off the team bus and everybody's getting onto elevators," Mazzone said.

"Well, don't go crazy."

"I'm fine," said Mazzone. "Don't worry. I'll get there."

"Have you got any questions?" Cox asked.

"Yeah, Bobby, I've got one. Who's the manager?"

"Me," replied Cox. The former manager-turned-GM was replacing Russ Nixon, who was fired after a 25–40 record that had the Braves in last place in the National League West.

"Oh, God, that's wonderful," Mazzone said. "I'll see you tomorrow at noon."

Mazzone had had designs on making it to the majors a different way. As a hard-throwing left-handed pitcher, he was signed out of high school by the Giants in 1967 out of Bruce High School in Westernport, Maryland. But he never rose above Triple A, spending ten seasons in the minors with San Francisco's and Oakland's systems, with whom he went 57–52 with a 3.64 ERA over 272 games.

Then during spring training in 1976, he received a call from A's farm director Syd Thrift. Mazzone's chances of pitching in the majors after a decade were slim. Instead he was offered a job managing Corpus Christi in the Lone Star League.

"I called him an unprintable word," Mazzone told the Associated Press in 1991. "I was basically lost. What was I going to do? If I can't pitch, I might as well shoot myself."

But he returned to Thrift's office the next day to apologize—and talk to him about the job.

Mazzone would win back-to-back independent league pennants in Corpus Christi before moving to Kinston in the Carolina League in 1978. Their owner, Ray Kuhlman, recommended Mazzone to the Braves, who made him a minor-league pitching coach.

It was there in 1979 that Mazzone would meet the man that would help to shape his philosophies on leading a staff—Richmond coach Johnny Sain.

"He was way ahead of his time," Mazzone said. "He was the first coach I ever talked to that didn't have the usual clichés."

The National League MVP runner-up in 1948 for the Braves, a rotation mate of the legendary Warren Spahn, and a three-time All-Star, Sain would go on to mold pitchers that helped claim World Series titles in 1961 and 1962 with the Yankees and with the Tigers in 1968. He had nine different pitchers win 20 games, among them Jim Bouton, Whitey Ford, Jim Kaat, Denny McLain, Earl Wilson, and Wilbur Wood.

But he was also outspoken and battled with managers, leading to his place in Triple A when Mazzone met him.

It was from Sain that Mazzone would learn the baseline for his pitcher's successes: throwing more often with less exertion. His pitchers threw from the mound as often as possible, but regulated their effort.

"Johnny was way ahead of his time, and I think that's why he moved around, four or five different teams and won everywhere he went, because his knowledge was so intimidating to the people that were in charge," Mazzone said, laughing.

"It's true. I saw in the minor leagues when Johnny was running the minor leagues and some people in the farm system at that particular time questioned his methods, and they had never really actually done anything."

If Mazzone was going to pick someone's brain, he was going to pick the brain of the man that had the most success of any pitching coach on the map.

Mazzone learned at the side of Sain, and Hank Aaron, the Braves' director of player development, allowed Mazzone to put his approach to work. A roving minor-league pitching instructor from 1979 to 1982, he was at Durham from 1983 to 1984 and Greenville—also in 1984 as manager—before he was brought up to be co–pitching coach in Atlanta with Sain, an experience he categorizes as a peacekeeping mission between Sain and manager Eddie Haas.

"It was the most humiliating, most embarrassing, most difficult year I ever spent in the game of baseball in my life," he told ESPN.com in 2005.

Mazzone returned to the minors, working in Sumter (1986), Greenville (1987), and in Richmond (1988–1990), where he'd receive that call in Buffalo on a night when one of his pitchers, Derek Lilliquist, had just tossed a shutout.

Mazzone had worked closely with Cox when he came back to Atlanta in 1986 as GM, the two discussing the development of the young arms in the minors—among them Glavine and Smoltz—and projecting rotations.

He trusted Mazzone's approach and the way he handled a staff, but the rocking? "He sometimes said it'd drive him crazy," Mazzone said.

When Mazzone arrived in Atlanta two months into the 1990 season, his first order of business was "get organized," he said, and he laid out what he wanted from his pitchers.

"All of us are going to be on the field at a particular time," he told them. "We are going to stay all on the field at the same time and we are going to leave the field at the same time."

He also implemented his throwing program. They would throw two bullpen sessions between starts instead of the one that every other team was doing, and they'd be throwing off the mound.

"I always encouraged them to throw, and not flat-footed throwing in the outfield, actually getting on a mound sixty-feet, six-inches and going downhill to a catcher," Mazzone said.

Tim Hudson, who was traded to the Braves before the 2005 season—Mazzone's last—immediately latched on to that idea.

"(That) makes all the sense in the world, because that's where you make pitches from is from the mound, from the slope," he said. "You don't try to make pitches from flat ground."

Mazzone remembers another pitching coach scoffing at the notion, telling him, "On the mound, they'll have a tendency to throw too hard."

"Aren't you being paid to regulate that?" Mazzone shot back.

There was another occurrence, this time with an opposing team executive, who couldn't believe the Braves' relievers followed the same plan.

"You can't do that," he told Mazzone. "What if he has to get in the game tonight?"

"What do you think we're preparing for?" Mazzone replied.

Like Sain before him, Mazzone had little patience for detractors or repeating himself during instruction.

"Leo would tell you one time," Perez said. "He'd tell you one time, 'You've got to do this, this and this' and that's it. If you didn't do it, he will get mad."

Smoltz was a believer in Mazzone after their first encounter in 1987, when the roving instructor didn't try to fix the right-hander's mechanics, but allowed him to throw in a way that felt most natural.

"I adapted right away," Smoltz said. "I felt so comfortable in that rotation and that type of bullpen [session]. I didn't know any different. I flourished and it kept me fresh and I thought that's the way everybody did it and come to find out, we were about the only ones that did that."

For all the fears of overexertion and injury from throwing more often, three Braves pitchers underwent Tommy John surgery during Mazzone's run: Kerry Ligtenberg in 1999, Smoltz in 2000, and Mike Hampton in 2005.

"There's more Tommy John surgeries than at any time in the history of baseball and that's the thing that we were most proud of," Mazzone said. "In our great run we didn't have any arm injuries, hardly to speak of."

Mazzone had a goal every spring that the Braves could get through the entire season with never having to change a pitcher because of injury.

"Leo," Schuerholz would tell him, "that's impossible."

"Well," Mazzone answered, "that's still my goal."

On September 10, 1993, Maddux took a line drive off his elbow and returned to the rotation eight days later. He was forced to skip a start, marking the first time since 1991 that one of the team's top four arms didn't make his assigned start.

The reason, Smoltz says, is "it really boils down to we never tapped out every pitch. We never exerted every pitch. We learned how to pitch."

And the results were immediate.

Last in the majors with a collective 4.58 ERA in 1990, the Braves—behind Mazzone's push to regulate effort and control the strike zone with that down and away fastball— shot up to third (3.49) during 1991's stunning run to the World Series, as Glavine won 20 games and his first Cy Young.

Over the next eleven seasons they would lead the majors in ERA eight times, including four in a row from 1997 to 2000, and finish second three times, including '94 (0.01 behind the Expos), '96 (the Dodgers won by .06), and '00 (.05 behind the Mariners).

"In our dynamic years of robust success, Leo got the job done," Schuerholz said.

It certainly helped having Glavine—who would have five 20-win seasons and add another Cy Young in 1998, Smoltz—the '96 Cy Young winner, and Maddux—the winner of that award from 1993 to 1995. But the true testament to Mazzone's ways is the impact he's had on the lesser names.

In 2000, the Braves picked up former All-Star John Burkett after he was cut by the Rays after spring training and coming off two seasons with ERAs of 5.62 and 5.68. By 2001 he was an All-Star again and was Atlanta's Opening Day starter with Maddux injured.

Likewise, Jaret Wright had fallen hard after starting Game Seven of the 1997 World Series for the Indians as a 21-year-old. In 2003 he had an 8.37 ERA in 39 games with the Padres, but Atlanta picked him up off waivers and he had a 2.00 ERA in 11 games and won 15 games in 2004 with a 3.28 ERA.

According to a breakdown of Mazzone's impact by economist J. C. Bradbury on his Sabernomics website, "working with Leo shaves off between .55 and .85 points of a pitcher's ERA. And I promise you, the results are not some artifact of some manipulation of the numbers to prove a point."

The Mazzone Effect, the man himself believes, isn't him doing something no one else is capable of. It's simply a matter of the way he approached his pitchers, treating them the same, whether it was Glavine, Maddux, Smoltz, Steve Avery, or Brad Clontz.

"If you have eleven pitchers on your staff and the number eleven guy is going to get the same amount of attention as your number-one guy, he's going to feel good about himself and feel important and when he's asked to contribute," Mazzone said.

Considered the best in the game, suitors came calling when Mazzone's contract was up in 2005. The Yankees were interested, but when good friend Sam Perlozzo, who had been named Orioles manager, pursued him, Mazzone couldn't pass up a homecoming.

"That's the only thing I've never second-guessed in my career," Mazzone said.

But he couldn't turn around Baltimore's staff, posting a 5.35 ERA in his first year—which was next-to-last in the majors—amid a 92-loss season. The following season the Orioles held that same ranking with a 5.17 ERA, and Mazzone was fired with one year remaining on his contract.

"My only regret is that I left and went to Baltimore and I should have stayed with the Braves and Bobby and coached my whole career there," he said. "That's the only thing I second-guess in my entire career."

In 2010, Mazzone threw his hat into the ring for openings to be the Mets' or Yankees' pitching coach, and after the '13 season he took to Twitter to lobby to fill the Phillies' vacancy.

He didn't get so much as an interview. At 67 and out of baseball, Mazzone finds himself in a similar spot to his greatest teacher, Johnny Sain, with a career arc that doesn't fit an unparalleled résumé.

"I think Leo and his philosophy needs to get back in baseball," Smoltz said.

Mazzone still has plenty of opinions on the state of the game, especially the growing emphasis on pitch counts—"I'm telling you, how pitchers are being handled in major league baseball is an insult. It really is," he said. "You're taking guys out after seven innings with 80, 90 pitches and they're dominating the game? They're not laboring. You could teach them how to finish games every once in a while to give your bullpen a break" —and has voiced them on local radio and during speaking engagements and clinics.

While Mazzone sits, waits, and rocks— "I'm rocking now talking to you," he said—the Braves have moved on with another accomplished arm whisperer.

Schuerholz had nearly two dozen names the organization was looking at as potential replacements for Mazzone when he left in 2005. But after a five-hour chat with the first one he and Cox interviewed, they realized they'd seen enough.

The Braves had their man.

"We almost thought there was no need to interview anyone else," Schuerholz told *USA Today* in 2006. "When you have a Hall of Fame manager say, 'I really like this guy,' you listen."

* * * *

Roger McDowell tapped a bat on the dugout floor as he motioned toward the string of fourteen consecutively numbered banners that run along the upper deck in

Turner Field's outfield.

"The fact that this organization was pitching-dominant and to have a kid from outside the organization . . . it was kind of like 'Why me? Why the outsider coming in?'" he said.

The bigger question, though, is whether anyone would have believed that the master of the hotfoot could have the organization put its faith in him fostering its pitching staff.

In a video from his late-80s Mets days, McDowell is joined by third baseman Howard Johnson, to, as McDowell puts it "introduce you to the wonderful world of hotfoot."

Johnson, at least, offers a disclaimer.

"This is not for you kids out there to try," he said. "This is done by experienced professionals."

The two display their craft as they wrap chewing gum around a roll of cigarettes. With the gum still in his mouth, McDowell spins the cigarettes in his finger, acting as a loom as he coats it.

"That's amazing," Johnson says. "How does he do it? How does he do it?"

"Mirrors," McDowell replies.

From there, the concept is simple: They crawl under the bench— "St. Louis is particularly good for that," McDowell notes, "because the bench is up high. It's like crawling in the rice fields, the patties"—tape it to the back of a teammate's shoe, and light it on fire.

McDowell can remember early in his career Mets manager Davey Johnson addressing his reliever's jokes and pranks, telling him "There's a time and a place, and make sure it's the right time, and make sure it's the right place."

That was McDowell's time and that was his place. At the helm of the Braves pitchers for more than a decade, he says he's still the same guy, but those around him have seen the changes as he transitioned from a player to a coach.

"He almost went the complete opposite to get rid of that perception he had as a player," said Gonzalez, Atlanta's manager since 2011. "He didn't want that to carry over to being a pitching coach. To this day, he is about as serious about his craft as I've ever seen anybody doing it."

Serious enough that when he decided to get into coaching, McDowell opted to start at the lower ranks.

He threw his last major-league pitch in 1996 at 35 with the Orioles. While he signed with the White Sox for 1997, two shoulder surgeries wiped out that year, and he retired after attending spring training in 1998.

For the next two years he flipped houses in California, where his wife, Gloria, was from.

"It was like, 'You know what? I love this,'" McDowell said. "But . . ."

He missed baseball. He found a way back in when he was visited by former teammate Jim Gott, who was doing community relations work for the Dodgers.

"You know what, why don't you start doing stuff with the Dodgers?" Gott told him. "I mean, they'll pay you a hundred bucks to go out and throw out the first pitch or go sign autographs or do whatever, but you get to go back to the ballpark and it's pretty cool."

McDowell did those appearances for a year and a half, but it wasn't enough. He couldn't do without the competition.

McDowell's mentor, Dave Wallace, who was then the Dodgers' assistant general manager and their former minor-league pitching coordinator, knew where he needed to be.

"I want to get back in the game, but I don't know what capacity, you know?" McDowell told him. "We had a daughter that was just born and I didn't want to spend time away from home. I didn't know if I was a scout . . ."

"I think you're best suited for on the field," Wallace told him.

The Dodgers hired McDowell, but he was clear that if he made it to the majors, he was going to earn it. He wasn't going to parlay his MLB service time into skipping levels as a coach.

"I think it was out of respect for the coaches at the major-league level," McDowell said, "because the coaches that I had throughout my major-league career had all been minor-league coaches before they got a major-league job—and it wasn't really en vogue to be a player, then go right into a big-league coaching job."

Said Gonzalez, "I respect him a lot for that, because you see guys that get done playing in the big leagues and they don't want to go to the minor leagues and coach."

In 2002, McDowell started with the low–Class-A South Georgia Waves in Albany, Georgia. Two years later he was promoted to the Triple-A Las Vegas 51s before the Braves came calling in October 2005.

Having already talked to the Mariners, and considered a candidate for the Dodgers' major-league job, McDowell impressed Cox and Schuerholz in his interview—which came three days after Mazzone left—so much, they wasted little time in hiring him.

"We moved as quickly as we did because we didn't want him to end up somewhere else," Schuerholz said at the time.

In the weeks before each spring training, Mazzone would hold an early pitching clinic that would be dubbed "Camp Leo." But upon his arrival, McDowell bristled at the notion that anyone would be referring to the continued use of that program as "Camp Roger."

"I said 'This is not about me,'" McDowell said. "'This is about getting pitchers ready for spring training and all those things.' I don't want to say trying to distance myself from Leo, but also trying to find my own niche, of what I thought would be, from a pitching standpoint, successful."

That included the two pillars of his approach: individualization, and the words of Wallace, which are the foundation of McDowell's philosophy:

They don't care how much you know until they know how much you care.

It's that tactic that he used when the Braves acquired Shelby Miller in a November 2014 trade with the Cardinals. He phoned the 24-year-old right-hander multiple times that winter, not to talk pitching, but to get to know him.

"We got to talk about his family and what he was doing for Christmas and all those things," McDowell said.

It was through those talks that he put Miller, who had been with St. Louis since being drafted in 2009, at ease even before he had shown up for spring training.

"All these things that are put on a new player's shoulders that you try to calm," McDowell said. "Maybe it's fear or maybe it's anxieties. 'Hey, enjoy. Come out here and enjoy. Get your work in, we're going to get our work in and enjoy being out here. That's what it's about.'"

McDowell can relate. He broke in with the Mets in 1985 and logged over 1,000 major-league innings while playing for five different organizations. Over his first five seasons he appeared in nearly 400 games, and in 1990 with the Phillies, he led the NL with 60 games finished.

"He got it," Hudson said. "He understood the battles guys went through every day and the struggles that guys may experience on a day-to-day basis and it was awesome. He was a guy that was really in your corner."

Part psychologist, McDowell shows them he cares by tailoring his tactics toward a player's interest. If they're into golf, he'll use golf analogies: "Where you use your lower-half legs to swing the club rather than your upper half," he said. "Visualize pitches like you visualize a shot in golf." Or if they're into fishing, he'll go that route: "You can use a fishing analogy as far as target, looking at your target." But by foregoing an overall philosophy, he can connect to each of his pitchers.

"Understand their background," he said. "Understand what makes them tick, what their interests are, what their family is, what do they like to do? When you find those things out, it makes the communication a lot easier."

Like Mazzone before him, McDowell has had his stars.

His pitchers have been responsible for ten of the Braves' representatives in the Midsummer Classic since 2006, a group that included Smoltz through his final All-Star season ('07) in Atlanta and an eventual 200-game winner in Hudson ('10). But he also fostered the talent of Craig Kimbrel, who McDowell helped turn into arguably the best closer of his generation, in representing the NL from 2011 to 2014, as well as Julio Teheran ('14) and Shelby Miller ('15), and helped Jonny Venters and Jair Jurrjens (both '11) perform at career levels.

And like Mazzone, McDowell has also proven adept at salvaging careers.

"He can do both, and that's what makes him special," Gonzalez said.

Aaron Harang finished fourth in the NL Cy Young voting in 2007, but from 2010 to 2013 he had a 4.36 ERA and joined the Braves as a 36-year-old who looked to be fading into retirement. But with McDowell in his ear, Harang rebounded with a 3.57 ERA and had 25 quality starts, which tied for second in the NL.

"One of the most important things that I learned from Bobby [Cox] was creating a comfortable environment, and the whole time I was here with Bobby—and, obviously before, because of all those banners—he created a comfortable environment for players," McDowell said. "I think that's very important in having a veteran pitcher come into your organization and making him feel comfortable."

The prankster isn't making any appearances in the Braves' dugout. McDowell's not holding any hotfoot tutorials or emerging from the clubhouse with his uniform on upside down.

There's no escaping his comedic past, though, as a reminder greets McDowell in his mailbox in the form of a check for $13.52.

He was at home in the winter of 1990 when a call came from former Mets teammate Keith Hernandez.

"Hey," Hernandez said. "Do you want to go to L.A. and be on *Seinfeld*?"

"Okay," McDowell said. 'What's *Seinfeld*?"

Hernandez knew creators and New Yorkers Jerry Seinfeld and Larry David, and McDowell had heard of the show, which had been on the air for a season, but he had never seen an episode.

"Yeah, okay," McDowell told him. "It's a trip to L.A. and I get to be on a TV show."

After arriving on set in the early morning—hours before the shoot—McDowell and Hernandez were talking to David and Seinfeld when the reliever watched a man walk up to the breakfast buffet that the catering service had set up.

"Does everybody get to eat here?" he asked David and Seinfeld.

"What do you mean?" they said.

"Like the janitor guy," McDowell answered, pointing to the man in line. "He looks like the janitor."

"No," they shot back, "that's Kramer."

Stunned that he didn't recognize actor Michael Richards, David asked McDowell, "You've seen the show, right?"

"Oh . . . yeah, yeah," McDowell replied. "I'm just kidding around."

More than two decades after it aired, he is still collecting royalty checks from that appearance in the second part of a two-episode arc entitled "The Boyfriend." In the episode, Kramer believes Hernandez spit on him after trash-talking the Met, but it's revealed—in a Zapruder film parody—that McDowell was the spitter, taking revenge on Kramer and Newman (Wayne Knight) for cursing at him and spilling beer on his head.

"I may get [a check] every couple of months and I might get two a month," McDowell said. "I guess it just depends on who picks it up and who shows it and where they show it.

"I had to be a card-carrying member of [the Screen Actors Guild] though. I had to join SAG, so I'm still a card-carrying member of SAG."

Chapter Twelve

John Schuerholz:
The Architect

The Royals were in a state of turmoil. John Schuerholz loved his job at a place he affectionately refers to as "the IBM of the American League: rock-solid, blue-chip, reliable." But the franchise was going through a transition in ownership and the general manager was stuck in the middle.

Aging owner Ewing M. Kauffman had taken on a partner in 1983 in Avron Fogelman, a Memphis-based, 45-year-old real estate mogul. He had purchased 49 percent of the team for $10 million and had an option to buy-out Kauffman entirely for an additional $10 million, no later than 1992.

Fogelman had designs on altering the way Kansas City operated, and he tabbed Schuerholz to put his vision into effect. It made him the poster boy for the changes in a front office that was still loyal to Kauffman and team president Joe Burke.

"It was a little instability going on," Schuerholz said.

Years later, with that negativity still brewing in Kansas City, Schuerholz was in New York for a meeting of MLB's Player Personal Development Program. A collection of owners, executives, and players' association members, they were working on a program to make opportunities available for MLBers after their careers were over.

"Many of them made monies, in those days not as much as they're making now, but they made a lot of money and they hadn't tended to that well," Schuerholz said. "They didn't have any plans for after-life professions or jobs or planning at all."

He was joined on that committee by Rangers owner and future forty-third president of the United States, George W. Bush, and Braves president Stan Kasten.

Their meetings concluded, and with time to kill before their flights, Schuerholz offered Kasten a ride to the airport in his rental car. Kasten had another idea: They could go to Yankee Stadium to catch a few innings beforehand.

During their drive to the Bronx, Kasten confided in Schuerholz. "I'm going to keep Bobby Cox in the dugout . . . and I'm looking for a general manager."

That previous June, Russ Nixon had been fired as manager and Cox, who was serving as GM, had taken on both roles. Kasten figured that Schuerholz, who had ten years in as the Royals' general manager, could be a resource.

"You're at the top of your game and you know a lot of guys," Kasten told him. "Think of any names, send them to me."

Schuerholz had helped turn the Royals into a force. He joined the expansion team in 1969, leaving behind the Orioles, whom he joined in 1966 after teaching at North Point Junior High in Baltimore. Working on a master's degree at Loyola University, he wrote a letter to Orioles owner Jerold Hoffberger that got his attention.

Less than three years later he was in Kansas City, serving as farm director, then scouting director and assistant GM before his promotion in the 1981 offseason made him the youngest general manager at 41.

Under his watch, the Royals finished lower than third in the American League West just once, and claimed three division titles and the 1985 World Series. He was part of the scouting department that drafted future Hall of Famer George Brett in the second round in 1971.

Schuerholz told Kasten he'd think about it and would get him a list of potential candidates, though there was one he kept coming back to: himself.

"Thought about it and thought about it and thought about it and things for me, personally, were altering the landscape in Kansas City, which was remarkable for most of my existence there," Schuerholz said.

When he returned to Atlanta he would call Kasten repeatedly, going over what he was looking for in a GM. Finally, after enough of those conversations, Kasten—who would later tell Schuerholz he wasn't baiting him with their initial talk—finally asked him.

"Are you interested in this job?"

"Maybe I am," Schuerholz replied.

On October 10, 1990, the 50-year-old was announced as the Braves GM, with Kasten saying, "I drew up a list of criteria and he was at the top of each individual measure. He was our number-one candidate. We got the very best guy we could and the only one I offered the job to."

Schuerholz was leaving what he calls "one of the most valued and appreciated and honored franchises in the American League" for a franchise that was an MLB-worst 65–97 the previous season, and which finished last in the National League West in four of the five previous seasons.

What, exactly, was he thinking?

"The world was shocked that I was leaving Kansas City to come here. The baseball world I guess," he said.

For those who were a part of that stunned segment of the population, Schuerholz would address it on the day of his hiring, and do so in his typically blunt fashion.

"Whatever horror stories you may have thought I've read or heard about the Braves, I have the confidence in my ability to get the job done," Schuerholz told reporters. "I'm not making any promises and there's no timetable. I don't believe in a quick fix."

Maybe he should have, bringing in key veterans that offseason to aid 1991's stunning run to the World Series. With Cox, Schuerholz would form one of the greatest manager/GM tandems the game has seen.

In John Schuerholz's first year as the Braves general manager they would start their streak of division titles. (*The SABR Office*)

That run of fourteen straight division crowns couldn't have happened without The Architect's ability to, year-in and year-out, maintain the Braves' core and add to it with youth and veterans.

"That, to me, has always been my view as a general manager for twenty-six years, that the best opportunity you have to put a winning team together and have it sustained over a long period of time, is to have the right mix of complementary players," Schuerholz said.

"Not an accumulation of individual star talent, people playing in different positions, but how they all mesh together. That was what I tried to do in all of my conversations with scouts, with everything I tried to do in putting together a team was about that."

During Schuerholz's run—which would last until October 12, 2007, when he stepped into the role of team president and was replaced by his assistant GM, Frank Wren—that may have been his biggest feat, maintaining that mix of continuity and new blood.

"It was a strategy, it was a plan. It was a process," he said from his office overlooking Turner Field. "We averaged ten new players a year throughout that run. It was easy to determine who your then-current core players were for a one- or two- or three-year period.

"You knew who were the most important elements of your team, who were productive, reliable, consistent, strong-willed, will to win, warriors, leadership, all those things. And it changed over time."

Pieces of that core were already in place from 1990 in the likes of Tom Glavine, John Smoltz, Steve Avery, Ron Gant, David Justice, and Mark Lemke. He would bolster that group with veterans Terry Pendleton, Sid Bream, Rafael Belliard, Charlie Leibrandt, Otis Nixon, and Deion Sanders that offseason, and add reliever Greg McMichael and deal for Alejandro Pena in-season.

"John Schuerholz had all those pieces there in the minor leagues and he knew how to put some veterans with that thing and he did it every year," Pendleton said. "He went out and made a deal to find that next guy to help us get to that next level or get us to the level we needed to be. It made it special. He knew what he was doing."

Over the years Greg Maddux would step in, while Bream and Pendleton stepped out. Javy Lopez and Ryan Klesko emerged and Otis Nixon moved on.

Mix in a free agent or big trade chip—see Fred McGriff—bring up a prospect or two, or three, but don't trade away valuable young players for veterans. That was one of the hallmarks of Schuerholz's time as GM, as the Braves bucked popular thinking and didn't shy away from allowing their prized prospects to take on key roles.

"Some guys' contracts ran out that we couldn't afford," Schuerholz said. "Some guys started to lose ability that we offloaded. Young guys moved into that," he said. "Somebody like Chipper Jones shows up and all of a sudden he's part of that core. It changed, but we knew, we identified well, mostly accurately, who that core was."

During that string of first-place finishes, only Smoltz would be a part of all fourteen teams. But the outside perception, because they would have a flow of pieces in that foundation that changed after a few years, was one of consistency.

"It seemed like it was a great deal of stability here, because we won every year," Schuerholz said, "and it seemed like the Braves played the same kind of baseball under the great leadership of Bobby Cox."

John Hart, now the Braves president of baseball operations, was Schuerholz's competitor during Hart's time in Cleveland—where he lost the 1995 World Series to Atlanta—and in Texas. He marvels at the longevity of the Braves' dominance in an era when so many teams are slaves to what he calls the "ebb and flow in every organization."

"I think it just shows how remarkable the run of the Braves was. I think any time you can jump out there and go five, six, seven years . . . that's a long window," Hart said. "To do it you have to have good, young players and you have to be wise in your free-agent acquisitions, and thirdly, I think you have to [add] small pieces to make a team work, where you bring new faces in, whether it's a couple bullpen guys, a utility infielder, an everyday guy, you make a deal for a starting pitcher—whatever it is."

By any measure, Schuerholz's time in Atlanta couldn't have started off any better.

On the field the Braves were a success, and after failing to attract one million fans to Atlanta–Fulton County Stadium the previous three seasons—they were the only MLB team to fall below that threshold—they drew over two million in 1991.

But from a personal standpoint, the move to Atlanta had its difficulties in the beginning. Schuerholz had spent twenty-three years in Kansas City and was leaving behind his wife, Karen, his young son, Jonathan, and a daughter, Gina, who was in her senior year of high school.

"You won't see me, so you might as well not see me in Kansas City while I'm in Atlanta," he told his wife.

He admits it was "lonely and it was tough" and he "wondered a lot of times why I left Kansas City, because we loved living there."

But what ultimately made the transition work were the relationships Schuerholz had forged.

He calls his conversations with Kasten "vibrant and exciting and fun and I was attracted to that" and lauds the efforts of Braves owner Ted Turner. By the time Schuerholz arrived, Turner had learned to step back in the daily operations of his franchise.

"I never had to convince anyone of anything," Schuerholz said. "That's not how it worked here . . . as general manager, I was completely in power."

Atlanta had rarely acted as a player on the free-agent market for years.

Blame an attempt to make a splash with a $44 million deal for Bruce Sutter in December 1984 that would see the Braves still paying him into the next millennium. The pitcher signed for a staggering thirty-six years, in a contract that paid him $750,000 a year for six years, then a minimum of $1.1 million for the following thirty years. It would be capped by a $9.1 million principal payment. But the first signs of life post-Sutter came in the form of Cox making his biggest splash with Nick Esasky, who signed for three years and $5.7 million in 1989. Esasky flamed out due to a battle with vertigo, but by the time Schuerholz was ready to add via free agency, Turner rarely batted an eye.

"He could have asserted that spirit and that part of his personality and said 'Nobody's more competitive than I am. Nobody wants to win more than I do. Nobody prepares more and wants it more than I did and I'm going to talk to Schuerholz about every one of these moves he's making,'" Schuerholz said. "[He] did not once [say that]. Every once in a while he would ask me to come to his office and we would chat . . . but he was remarkably smart, asked all the right questions, and took your answer for what you were offering and didn't contest it."

Turner would invite the Schuerholzes and Cox and his wife, Pam, to go hunting with him in Florida, New Mexico, and South Carolina. It didn't happen often, but Schuerholz simply says, "it was a great relationship."

But Schuerholz didn't operate in a vacuum, often pulling together the coaching staff for a sit-down meeting before making a move. If someone had enough concerns

about a player or a direction, the GM wasn't above changing his course.

"He was able to sit and listen, and [just] because he
was just the chief and boss he wouldn't [simply] do what
he wanted to do," Pendleton said. "He valued every guy's
opinion at that table when we had the coaching staffs in
the early nineties. He valued their opinions on what might
need to be done, what we could do to get better and if we
could get better."

Schuerholz's dealings with Turner, Kasten, and the
coaching staff helped to build the environment of the organization, but no relationship loomed larger than the one
he had with Cox.

They had already known each other from when the
manager was with the Yankees and Schuerholz was GM in
Kansas City. The two saw each other at the Winter Meetings or at a game and would occasionally get together afterward.

"Didn't know each other well, but knew each other
enough to be able to sit down and have a postgame drink,
talk about baseball, talk about what's going on in our organizations, what's going on in the game," Schuerholz said.

It was enough that they had a mutual respect before
they began a working relationship. It helped that they
found out they were very much in line when it came to the
kind of players they wanted to pursue.

Be it the veterans they added before their first season
together in 1990 or the likes of Maddux in 1992 and Mc-
Griff a year later, the tandem of Cox and Schuerholz were
weighing character as much as on-field ability.

"Bobby was a good judge of talent and a good judge
of people," Schuerholz said. "I believed that I was, that I
was a good judge of talent and a good judge of a person
and how that person would fit into what we had in place or
what it was that we desired to create in this place.

"He and I very, very seldom differed on that. Every once in a while we did because we're humans and we have different thoughts and ideas. But not very often in terms of the character of the person we wanted to represent us, to wear our uniform and try to win games and pennants for us."

Schuerholz had a knack for trading prospects or marginally producing players for stars, highlighted by the 1993 deal that brought back McGriff from the Padres for Donnie Elliott, Vince Moore, and Melvin Nieves; also in '95 when the Braves sent the Expos a package of Esteban Yan, Roberto Kelly, and Tony Tarasco for Grissom.

Why were teams willing to send proven major-league players, and in essence, help keep the Braves at the top of the baseball universe? Schuerholz believes they simply wanted a taste of what Atlanta was developing in the minors.

"We were viewed as an organization, and rightly so, that was rich and flush with talent up and down the system and put us in a great, strong position from which to make a deal, to negotiate a deal, to put deals together," Schuerholz said. "People were attracted to Atlanta Braves' minor-league players, young players, even some that had matriculated through to the major leagues and had become starters, but their talent was analyzed and valued. It wasn't that we were tricking people."

But Schuerholz's strategies weren't always perfect.

Deion Sanders's persona didn't always mesh with the professionalism of the clubhouse in his four seasons in Atlanta. The most glaring incident came at the expense of CBS's Tim McCarver, with the broadcaster criticizing Sanders for playing for the NFL's Falcons and the Braves the same day.

McCarver was promptly doused with ice water in the celebration after Game Seven of the 1992 NLCS. Then Sanders did it again. And again. "He tried to hit me with another tub that missed me, and I said, 'You know, Deion, you're a real man, you are a real man,'" McCarver told the *Los Angeles Times*. "I thought it was a deliberate, cowardly act."

"Every once in a while we'd try a wild card," Schuerholz said. "We'd get somebody who had overwhelming ability and whose past circumstances put up red flags about their makeup and how they fit with the team, and so on and so forth. If it didn't work we invited them to leave. But we tried. But not often."

In 1997 he sent Jermaine Dye to the Royals along with Jamie Walker for Michael Tucker and Keith Lockhart, a deal that came two days after shipping Justice and Marquis Grissom to the Indians for Kenny Lofton and Alan Embree. Tucker was gone after two uneventful seasons, and while Lockhart supplied 59 pinch hits in six seasons in Atlanta, Dye was a World Series MVP, two-time All-Star, and a Gold Glove and Silver Slugger Award winner.

After the 2003 season the Braves sent one of their top pitching prospects, Adam Wainwright, to the Cardinals along with Jason Marquis and reliever Ray King, in exchange for J. D. Drew. Marquis made an All-Star team, King pitched for 10 seasons, and Wainwright would become a multiple-time All-Star and Gold Glove winner.

Drew and the Braves were unable to agree upon an extension and he left for the Dodgers as a free agent.

In 2007, Schuerholz acquired power-hitting first baseman Mark Teixeira from the Rangers for a haul that included future Rookie of the Year Neftali Feliz; All-Stars Elvis Andrus and Matt Harrison; and Jarrod Saltalamacchia, who has spent a decade in the majors.

With Teixeira headed to free agency after the following season, the Braves flipped him to the Angels after 157 games in Atlanta for first baseman Casey Kotchman and pitching prospect Stephen Marek.

That would be the last trade that Schuerholz would make as GM, as he informed team chairman and CEO Terry McGuirk after the 2007 season that he wanted to be a senior advisor. McGuirk would come back days later and make him the Braves president. In announcing the move, McGuirk said Schuerholz "will be my right-hand man" in regards to all of the team's operations, both on and off the field.

There were misses, but they come with the territory. It was obviously the hits and the longevity that should see Schuerholz join the growing number of Braves in Cooperstown.

Current manager Fredi Gonzalez sums up what Schuerholz has meant to the organization with just one word:

"Stability."

Since World War II, only eight manager/general manager combinations have been together for more than eleven years. It's an impressive group, including the Cardinals' Tony La Russa and Walt Jocketty, the Dodgers' Walter Alston and Buzzie Bavasi (and later Tommy Lasorda and Al Campanis), the Giants' Bruce Bochy and Brian Sabean, the Pirates' Danny Murtaugh and Joe L. Brown, and the Yankees' Casey Stengel/George Weiss and Joe Torre/ Brian Cashman.

And, of course, Cox and Schuerholz.

"I think where people make mistakes, where organizations make mistakes in all aspects, whether in business or sports, is that constant change," Gonzalez said. "Presidents, managers, general managers, there's never any voice. It's a different dynamic every two years or three years.

"Look at the organizations that have done well for a long time. . . . All those organizations that have been successful is because of the constants of their leadership team."

There are thirty-three pioneers and executives in the Hall of Fame, but only four of them were team architects for the majority of their careers—Ed Barrow, Pat Gillick, Branch Rickey, and George Weiss. But only one of them—Gillick in 2012—has been inducted in the past forty-five years.

Gillick won division titles for four different franchises (Blue Jays, Mariners, Orioles, and Phillies) and three World Series titles (two in Toronto and one in Philadelphia). But it's Schuerholz—the winningest GM in the game's history—that is the measuring stick for the position in this era, and it wasn't just his sixteen division titles, six pennants, and two World Series wins in all that underscore that claim.

It was how he did it and the era he accomplished it in.

Cashman has his argument as the era's best, with four World Series titles and seven AL pennants on his résumé, but the Yankees stopped at nine straight division crowns in his tenure—and there was always the will of owner George Steinbrenner weighing over his biggest decisions. There's a reason he's been referred to as a personal shopper.

Jocketty was also a model of consistency with his seven NL Central titles in St. Louis, two pennants, and a World Series title. But in 1994 he inherited a franchise that had experienced just two losing seasons in its previous thirteen years and made three Series in that span. The Braves had one division title in twenty-one years before Schuerholz's arrival.

The A's Billy Beane started a revolution by exploiting inefficiency in the market to spawn Moneyball, but for all that he's meant to the practical implementation of sabermetrics, Oakland hasn't gone past the ALCS on his watch.

"Because of the pressure to win and GMs becoming so vulnerable you're seeing a lot more decisions that are short-term oriented," former Astros GM Gerry Hunsicker told the *Dallas Morning News* in 1996. "You're seeing a gotta-win-today mentality, instead of rebuilding and the lag time that goes with it."

The most impressive part of Schuerholz's time as GM is that, somehow, he managed to do both.

He rarely lacked for financial support in his reign, with Atlanta having a top-five payroll five times, including 1994 when it topped the majors at $49.38 million, but the Braves weren't free-spenders, topping $100 million just once at $106.2 million in 2003.

For seven straight seasons (2001–2007), the Yankees averaged $168 million, including payrolls of $208 million ('05) and $207 million ('07).

Schuerholz also has the admiration of his fellow GMs, like Hart.

"I came, frankly, not only to admire what he's done professionally, but to love him as a man," Hart said. "I think he's just a terrific individual, very smart . . . he's got it wired down."

Schuerholz may not have been responsible for Tom Glavine's, John Smoltz's, or Chipper Jones's paths to Atlanta, but it was his maneuvers that pushed the Braves to an elite level and kept them there for nearly a decade and a half.

His Hall of Fame fate rests in the hands of the Expansion Era Committee, which meets every three years. Their next scheduled meeting is at the 2016 Winter Meetings, where they'll consider candidates for the 2017 class. With four Braves—Cox, Glavine, Maddux, and Smoltz—in the 2014 and 2015 classes, Schuerholz may suffer from Braves fatigue, delaying his election.

But by all accounts, it's coming, some day.

"To John Schuerholz," Cox said in his own HOF induction speech in 2014, "the general manager—now president of the Braves—who gave us the players we needed to win fourteen straight division titles. I could only say 'Hope to see you here soon, John.'"

As Schuerholz told reporters after a 2004 visit to the Hall ahead of a matchup with the Twins in the now-defunct Hall of Fame Game, "Baseball is in my marrow and this place was created for all of us that have a love affair with the game. There's no better place to celebrate that passion than in the epicenter of baseball, which is here."

Years before he and Kasten ever talked about the Braves' GM opening, Schuerholz was at one of his lunches with Burke and fellow front-office member Herk Robinson.

Their conversations would run the gamut of baseball, and one topic would prove prophetic.

"One of the things we'd talk about is, where are towns in major-league baseball that have the capacity and possibility of being dynamic? That something's missing in those towns," Schuerholz recalls.

The two cities they agreed upon: Dallas and Atlanta. Both, they surmised, were big communities that could succeed with the right philosophies and the right team in place.

Schuerholz's thoughts went back to that when Kasten's offer came.

"I said 'I'm going to do this,'" he said.

It's a marriage that has him nearing a milestone. The 2016 season, he happily announces, is his 75/50/25 year. He'll be 75 years old, in his fiftieth year in baseball and the twenty-fifth with the Braves.

Schuerholz wrote a poem in tribute to Royals manager Dick Howser, who died in June 1987 of a brain tumor. It opens with legendary managers Walter Alston, Connie Mack, and Casey Stengel welcoming Howser to heaven, and includes a line that may end up summarizing Schuerholz's own career.

They'll pull another chair up to the heavenly hot-stove table because they know their newest brother is among the very able.

Chapter Thirteen

Arrival and Departure of the Baby Braves

At the mention of the now infamous *Sports Illustrated* cover, Tim Hudson can't help but break into a smirk of a smile.

"You know what," the former Braves right-hander said, "that was pretty funny."

There was rookie Jeff Francoeur on the magazine's August 26, 2005, edition, with Turner Field as a backdrop. He gazed into the camera, grinning, with the headline "The Natural."

He was the rock star of Atlanta's youth movement, taking the city and baseball by storm as part of the eighteen rookies dubbed the Baby Braves who would help key the last of the franchise's unparalleled fourteen consecutive division crowns.

But that didn't mean the veterans in the clubhouse weren't going to have a little fun with the 21-year-old.

"So we busted his chops a little bit about that," Hudson said. "We even actually got one of his bats and drew a lightning bolt down the side of it and put 'Roy Hobbs' on it and made him take (batting practice) with it a couple of games."

No stadium lights were harmed—à la Robert Redford in the 1984 film's climax—and neither was the young outfielder's ego.

"[Hudson would] make him do all kinds of stuff," said Fredi Gonzalez, who was the third-base coach that season. "He handled it really, really well."

SI had only wheeled that headline out once before—when it put a 20-year-old Ken Griffey Jr. on its May 7, 1990, cover—and Francoeur's start seemed to herald the similar arrival of one of the game's newest stars.

Only this story was even better, the embodiment of the cliché "local boy makes good."

Less than thirty miles from where the Braves were rattling off titles was where Francoeur was doing the same for Lilburn, Georgia,'s Parkview High School.

He claimed two baseball state championships in 2001 and 2002, hitting .443 with 55 home runs in four years. In the Georgia 5A finale vs. Lassiter as a senior, Francoeur went 6-for-7 with four home runs in the series, two doubles, a walk, seven RBIs, and five runs scored. He also picked up the win in both games, coming on in relief.

Francoeur also won a pair of football titles as a defensive back and wide receiver, setting school records with 47 receptions and 15 interceptions in 2000 and as a senior had 1,033 receiving yards. During his junior and senior seasons, the Panthers went 30–0 and he ended his career as Georgia's high school player of the year.

The 6-foot-4, 205-pounder was rated as a four-star prospect by Rivals.com and the eleventh-ranked safety in the Class of 2002. At the position he came in ahead of former All-ACC pick Brandon Meriweather of Miami and Virginia Tech's unanimous All-American Jimmy Williams.

Francoeur was heavily recruited, drawing interest from the likes of Clemson, Georgia Tech, Mississippi State, North Carolina, and Vanderbilt—and even set off a bit of a feud between Clemson's coach, Tommy Bowden, and his legendary father, Florida State's Bobby.

"He was a great safety," Bowden said. "He's a guy that could have played wide receiver, could have played safety, might have grown into a linebacker . . . he would have been an inside receiver. There were four positions he could have played."

While Tommy was at the Francoeurs for dinner on his official visit—chicken Parmesan and shrimp—the elder Bowden called. His son picked up the phone and hung up on him.

The idea Tommy Bowden and the Tigers' baseball coaches were pitching was Francoeur could play both football and baseball for the ACC school. There was always the threat he would pursue a professional baseball career, but Bowden saw value in chasing Francoeur.

"I felt pretty confident he'd [be picked] in baseball," Bowden said. "But what happens in recruiting, you sign a great player, it gets contagious, and all of a sudden he'll pull somebody else in."

Or, as Bowden recalls telling Francoeur, "I don't care if you come or not. You're going to help us."

He signed his letter of intent, and an image on Clemson's official site shows Francoeur standing at a locker bearing his name, wearing a number 12 jersey.

With his help, the Tigers brought in the fourth-rated class in the conference that year per Rivals, a haul that also included future first-round NFL pick Gaines Adams.

"We were very pleased to get him," Bowden said of Francoeur.

But then the Braves entered the mix.

They claimed the local product with the twenty-third overall pick in the 2002 draft, taking him two picks before the Giants grabbed future All-Star Matt Cain. But with the leverage of his scholarship in hand, it was no given Francoeur would sign.

"We still have to negotiate the contract," Francoeur told MLB.com in 2002. "I'm still prepared to go to Clemson if we can't work something out."

The Braves weren't willing to lose him, giving Francoeur the biggest signing bonus in franchise history at $2.2 million.

A little more than three years later, he was *Baseball America*'s third-rated outfield prospect, and with right fielder Brian Jordan on the 15-day disabled list with left knee discomfort, the call came for Francoeur—who had hit 13 home runs in 335 at-bats for Double-A Mississippi—on July 6, 2005.

He rushed to his parents' home from Montgomery, Alabama, returning at 1:00 a.m., and hours later was walking into the Braves clubhouse for the first time for a doubleheader against the Cubs.

Luckily for the star-struck Francoeur—seeing the likes of Chipper Jones, Andruw Jones, and John Smoltz—he sat out the opening game.

"It was surreal that first game, seeing those guys," he said.

Francoeur started the second game, grounding out to third base on a 1–1 pitch by Jerome Williams in his first at-bat and following with strikeouts in the fourth and sixth. But then in the eighth with Roberto Novoa on the mound, he sent a towering shot to center field to score three runs.

"Jeff Francoeur's first big-league hit, a bomb," Chip Caray called out on the broadcast.

The camera cut to his parents, both of whom are middle school teachers, and Skip Caray added, "David and Karen can't believe it. You know when your kid does well in Little League? Well, this is that times about a hundred thousand."

Let the hype begin.

In his first fourteen games, Francoeur hit six home runs with 16 RBIs and carried a .405 average, which at the time made him the only active player with that many runs driven in his first fourteen games.

Though there was at least one thing he seemingly couldn't do.

When the Braves left for his first career road trip to face the Mets—which would lead to a bit of irony for Francoeur—he didn't know how to tie his tie. So he asked play-by-play announcer Chip Caray to show him.

"He's going to be a superstar, no doubt about it," Chipper Jones told MLB.com. "He'll be the next Dale Murphy in this city."

Said Hudson, "Frenchy came up and he took the league by fire for a while. He was having a lot of success."

With it came a loss of anonymity, and while he was used to being a bit of a celebrity, this was amplified.

"When you're sitting there at twenty-one years old, driving down to Turner Field and driving home after, you're going to a bar or anything and just people recognize [you] and tell you 'Great job. Keep it up,'" Francoeur said. "As a twenty-one-year-old, it can be overwhelming, to be honest with you."

There were more demands for his time: a commercial here, a photo shoot there, and even the Braves would ask him to pose for ads.

He did a Delta commercial in which he reads a letter from a Braves fan in Copenhagen, then proceeds to go out onto the field and hit a signed ball that falls into the child's glove. In Denmark. At the end, the camera cuts back to show a bucket of balls labeled for Europe, South America, and Africa.

It began to eat into his pregame work, and Gonzalez pulled Francoeur aside to make sure the late-arriving phenom was keeping it all in perspective.

"Hey, you do what you want," Gonzalez told him, "but make sure you do your work here first. Because if you hit .190 and you get sent down to the minor leagues, those billboards, they're gone."

But it all seemed to come so easy for Francoeur, who remembers thinking, "Man, it can't be this easy. You're going to have to make adjustments."

Only, one month in, he was still over .400—.403 to be exact, prompting that tag line on his *SI* cover, which said, "Atlanta rookie Jeff Francoeur is off to an impossibly hot start. Can anyone be this good?"

"At that point . . . you're just living in the moment," he said. "You're just enjoying every day, every hit, every win. Eventually you've got to make adjustments and do that, but at that point in my career and where we were at, I was just every day loving it."

It helped staying grounded that Francoeur wasn't the only rookie in Atlanta—the outfielder made it ten—nor was he the lone product of the metro area.

The Braves had three other players who were raised in the suburbs in catcher Brian McCann (Duluth) and pitchers Kyle Davies (Decatur) and Blaine Boyer (Marietta).

"We all came up at the same time," McCann said. "We were all young. We were thrown into a pennant race and we were big contributors to the reason that we won."

When Francoeur reached home after hitting that debut home run, it was McCann who greeted him. The two bumped chests and Francoeur slapped the catcher on the top of his helmet.

McCann, 21, also began the season in Double A. And like Francoeur, he also made the most of his first appearance in a Braves uniform, getting two hits on June 10 against the Athletics.

Francoeur and McCann had known each other since they were kids, playing on the same teams since they were 12 years old. The two lived together their first two seasons in the majors, though their hands were forced there. Initially, Francoeur and McCann were still living with their parents and were fined $50 each day by the kangaroo court until they would move out.

"We figured it would be cheaper to go get an apartment," Francoeur said.

Hudson chuckled thinking back on it, saying, "They were young enough where they were probably staying in their high school bedroom. I'm sure Francoeur still probably still had his Chipper Jones poster up in his bedroom."

As Jordan put it, "We had to make them grow up fast. Separate, get out of your mom's stomach. You're done. We always had fun with it."

Brad McCann—Brian's older brother and an All-American third baseman at Clemson, who would go on to be picked by the Marlins in the sixth round in 2004—lived with them too. They'd make Taco Bell runs at 2:00 a.m., play Mario Kart until 5:00 a.m. and, basically, "Do what any twenty-one-, twenty-two-year-old guy would do," Francoeur said.

That offseason the trio, along with the matching Cavalier King Charles spaniels that Francoeur and the younger McCann bought, would move into a house in a Lawrenceville subdivision that the catcher had purchased. They added Ping-Pong and a pool table, which they kept in the living room.

"We happened to be together all the time, so pretty much every day—and Brian wasn't very big into golf then—when I played golf we weren't really together, but besides that we were together all the time," Francoeur said.

Including on the field, as within two weeks of his arrival, Francoeur and McCann were among the rookies earning starts, along with third baseman Wilson Betemit (filling in for an injured Chipper) and right fielder Kelly Johnson.

Johnson would later recall a victory in Cincinnati in which the Braves ended the game with five rookies on the field at once.

"We were slapping hands at the end and I remember McCann looking at me and saying, 'Can you [expletive] believe this?'" he said.

The Braves clubhouse, despite featuring two franchise icons from the 1995 World Series team—Chipper Jones and Smoltz—was seen as button-downed, and in need of some enthusiasm.

They got it via the Baby Braves.

"There's no questioning the enthusiasm of McCann, the enthusiasm of Francoeur, the quiet professionalism of Kelly Johnson," said Chip Caray. "All those things kind of rubbed off. It was the perfect mix of young and old and guys in between, like Chipper Jones. It was really a terrific blend that year."

It helped having Andruw Jones rip off a career season. Arguably the greatest center fielder of his generation, as he won ten straight Gold Gloves he led the majors in homers in 2005 and finished second to the Cardinals' Albert Pujols in the MVP voting.

"Of course, Andruw Jones went from hitting 12 home runs through two months to ending with [51]; that had something to do with it," Johnson said. "But we won the division."

Patience was also key.

Johnson would start his career 1 for 30 at the plate, but Bobby Cox kept trotting him out there, starting nine of his first 11 games. Johnson would find his way, hitting .265 the rest of the regular season and started all but eleven games from June 13 on. He ended the year at .241 with nine homers and 40 RBIs.

Meanwhile, Davies went 7–6 with a 4.93 ERA in 21 games, second baseman Pete Orr turned in a .300 season at the plate, outfielder Ryan Langerhans hit .267 with eight homers and 42 RBIs, Betemit hit .305, and relievers Boyer

Future All-Star Brian McCann was one of the 18 rookies who helped the Braves to a 14th straight division crown in 2005. (*Keith Allison*)

(4–2, 3.11 ERA), Macay McBride (5.79 ERA in 23 games), and Roman Colon (5.28 ERA over 23 games).

All figured prominently, but along with Francoeur's star turn, it was McCann that set the tone for what was to come.

He hit .278/.345/.400 with five homers and 23 RBIs in 180 at-bats and would become the only Brave to homer in his first postseason at-bat as he took the Astros' Roger Clemens deep for a three-run shot in Game Two of the National League Division Series.

"He had that hunger in his eyes and in his face that said, 'You know what, I might have just gotten called up from Double-A, but I'm a badass whether you know it or not,'" Hudson said.

Early on, Hudson marveled at McCann's ability to understand the strengths and weaknesses of his pitchers. It was beyond his twenty-one years.

"You try to figure out what the hitter's weaknesses are and try to figure out how that pitcher is going to come out there and how are we going to exploit those weaknesses," Hudson said. "He was a guy that was able to understand that at an early age."

On the night the Braves clinched the division title, with a 3-2 win over the Rockies on September 27—they would finish two games ahead of the Phillies at 90–72— the 38-year-old Smoltz put it all into perspective.

"We did it with six, twelve, fourteen rookies," he said in his postgame interview. "Tomorrow, they're going to be watching Bugs Bunny."

Rookies, twelve of whom made their debuts that season, would end up supplying 30 percent of the at-bats.

Going out with the old and in with the new could lead to hard feelings, but Jordan, who gave way to Francoeur, applauds the way the young players gelled with the older ones.

"Those guys were so easy to get along with," he said. "They were like sponges. They just wanted to learn and get better, so it was fun for me. "Even though Jeff Francoeur eventually took my position in right field, I didn't mind. I was about winning and he had a lot of talent. For me, I'm a competitor, but by me playing so he learned a lot. He learned when I get in there and I want that position, I've got to do it every day. To me all those guys are better off."

During the locker room celebration of the division crown, Rafael Furcal watched from afar. He couldn't be around alcohol while on probation for a drunken-driving charge, and after the champagne and beer bottles had been emptied, the players grabbed Furcal and using Diet Cokes and Sprites, doused him.

"It was a really tight, close-knit group," said Chip Caray.

And amid that atmosphere, the young players didn't waste the opportunity to learn from the players they grew up idolizing.

"I think for all of us—I speak for all the Baby Braves when we came up—we got a chance to pick Chipper Jones's brain and Smoltzy and we were thrown into the fire and we all responded well," McCann said.

Eight of those rookies made that postseason roster, but the energy and enthusiasm they brought to the locker room couldn't keep the Braves from bowing out in the opening round for the fourth straight year. They lost to the eventual NL champion Astros 4–0.

But as they gathered for the team photo to commemorate the division win, first base coach Glenn Hubbard summed up the impossibility of it all.

"This is the Braves' finest hour," he told Cox News Service. "This one is better than any of those others . . . except maybe the 1991 one, but it's right there."

From that Worst-to-First season on, the foundation of the Braves' run had been the stars it produced. With these additions it was hard to believe that the franchise had simply turned the page, subbing in the next wave of stars.

"You felt like it, at least I did," said Chip Caray. "You have to really guard yourself against that, because when you see young players, the history of our game is littered with guys who come in, make big impacts, and fade into oblivion, and it happens a lot."

It's a lesson that Francoeur would come to embody.

In his first full season, Francoeur was clearly at home and at ease with his place as a centerpiece of the franchise. During 2006 spring training he and Smoltz played golf together twenty-two days straight.

"I basically just packed my clubs every day, headed to the field, and after that get ready to [golf]," he said.

But he took a step back on the field, hitting .260, and struck out 132 times while drawing just 23 walks. His 3.4 percent walk rate was the third-worst among qualified players, and only seven left fielders had a higher K-rate than his 19.2. He did hit 29 home runs, though, and supplied 103 RBIs.

Meanwhile, McCann turned in his first All-Star season with a .333/.388/.572 slash line, 24 homers, 93 RBIs, and won a Silver Slugger Award.

That next spring, the Braves signed McCann to a six-year, $27.8 million contract extension and many believed with him locked up, they could do the same for Francoeur.

But after presenting the right fielder and his agent, Steve Hammond, with a deal reportedly in line with McCann's, the Braves received a counteroffer. It was nearly double.

He answered his contract dispute by winning his first Gold Glove in '07 and hitting .293 with a career-high 105

RBIs and .782 OPS. But a year later, he was slumping again (.239 average and 11 homers in 653 plate appearances) and was demoted to Double A for three games.

That offseason he sought out the help of Rangers hitting coach Rudy Jaramillo, but after five homers, 35 RBIs, and a .250 average to start '09, the Braves had seen enough.

Before the second game of a four-game road trip in Denver to end the season's first half, Francoeur got called into Cox's makeshift office in Coors Field.

He was being traded to the Mets for Ryan Church, another outfielder in need of a change of scenery.

But in a cruel twist of fate and scheduling, New York's first road trip of that second half of the season was in Atlanta—for a four-game series.

"It sucked. Because, if you think about it, it was like I would have been back here like any other Brave, because we were on the road, then it's the All-Star break and you're here," Francoeur said. "It wasn't a lot of fun, to come back your first time and see all those guys, you were just with them in the locker room less than a week ago."

Francoeur struggled to start that series, going a combined 0-for-7 in the first two games, but rebounded with three hits in the next two and added two RBIs. Years later it's an experience he would just as soon forget.

"I'll be honest with you, of all the times I've had in baseball, the least fun four days was coming back here so quick," he said. "It was just too fresh."

He wasn't the first of the Baby Braves to be dealt— that was Betemit, who was shipped to the Dodgers in 2006. A year later, Davies (Royals) and McBride (Tigers) were dealt and Orr was released, then in '08, Devine was traded to Oakland and Brayan Pena was put on waivers and claimed by the Royals.

Johnson would leave via free agency in 2009, signing with the Diamondbacks, leaving only McCann.

In 2015, Johnson returned, making the team as a non-roster invitee before he was then flipped to the Mets in July (on the same weekend that former teammate Smoltz was inducted into the Hall of Fame). It was McCann, though, that would be the longest tenured of that group of eighteen rookies by far.

He was a seven-time All-Star in nine years in Atlanta, claiming five Silver Sluggers, and hit at least 20 home runs in each of his last six seasons. But after the 2013 season, with catcher Evan Gattis on the roster and highly touted prospect Christian Bethancourt in the wings, the Braves let McCann walk.

He signed a five-year, $85 million contract with the Yankees and continued to be one of the most consistent catchers in history with two more 20–home run seasons. Johnny Bench, Yogi Berra, Gary Carter, and Mike Piazza are the only other players at the position to have nine or more 20-homer seasons.

As McCann headed to Turner Field in 2015, he made a drive he'd made so many times before from his suburban Atlanta home. But when he walked into the stadium, some of those familiar feelings disappeared.

"It felt different coming into the other side, going into the visitor's clubhouse for the first time," he said. "Never been in there."

Playing in the park for the first and only time as a visitor—the Braves are headed to SunTrust Park in 2017 and with Atlanta not facing the American League East again until their move—he sat in the dugout before a throng of reporters, reflecting on where it all began.

"I remember it like it was yesterday," he said.

McCann is working on a résumé that should put him into the Hall of Fame discussion. As for his old roommate, he may not have lived up to the unfair bar his first months in the league created, but Francoeur has carved out an enviable career.

He's spent more than a decade in the game, with stops in New York, Texas, Kansas City, San Francisco, San Diego, and Philadelphia following his time in Atlanta.

Sure, there's always hindsight, where he wishes that storybook start to his time in a Braves uniform could have continued. But . . .

He flashes that smile—the one *SI* helped make famous—and the aw-shucks look that remains a staple into his thirties.

"At the same time, I got to play in New York, I got to go to a World Series with Texas," he said. "[If I would have stayed in Atlanta,] I would have missed a lot of cool things I would have been able to experience too."

Chapter Fourteen

The Braves Way

The Braves had lost their way.

More to the point, they had lost the Braves Way, and a triumvirate of the franchise's past, present, and future sat together at a table during a September 2014 press conference in the bowels of Turner Field to take the first step in regaining it.

"The Braves Way has been the organization's philosophy for many, many years," said team president John Schuerholz, who was joined by Hall of Fame manager Bobby Cox and interim general manager John Hart. "Bobby and I, working together for seventeen years as general manager and manager, lived the Braves Way every day. People in our organization, in the farm department, scouting organization, lived the Braves Way.

"It is our goal and our emphasis to find that Braves Way again."

Atlanta was in the midst of a late-season collapse, going from half a game ahead of the Nationals in the National League East on July 29 to 17 games back by season's end.

That fall included an eight-game losing streak and a 7–18 September.

GM Frank Wren, Schuerholz's former right-hand man, was the fall guy, responsible for a $112 million payroll that stood as the largest in franchise history, including $14 million to his free-agent signing B. J. Upton (.198/.279/.314 in two seasons)—who in 2012 signed the largest free-agent contract in Braves history at five years, $75 million—and $13 million to Dan Uggla, who had been released that July.

Wren had also inked third baseman Chris Johnson—who was coming off a career year in 2013—to a three-year, $23.5 million extension that would kick in beginning in 2015. But '14 was the worst of his six years in the majors with a .235 average and a career-high 159 strikeouts.

Add in that outfielders Jason Heyward and Justin Upton—both with 20 home run/20 stolen base seasons under their belts—were a year away from free agency (and expected to command upwards of $150 million or beyond), an all-or-nothing offensive approach that led to 4,042 strikeouts from 2012–2014—second highest in the majors behind the Astros' 4,342—and a farm system that *Baseball America* ranked 29th, and the Braves' leadership group had seen enough.

"It was time. It was time for the organization's well-being," Schuerholz said at the press conference announcing Wren's dismissal.

Less than a year earlier, Wren sat at the same table in the same room alongside 24-year-old All-Star first baseman Freddie Freeman, the sides having agreed to an eight-year, $135 million contract. It was the longest deal in Braves history, eclipsing the six-year, $90 million given to Chipper Jones in 2000.

Weeks later, at the team's spring training complex at Walt Disney World's Wide World of Sports, came a barrage of extensions.

Closer Craig Kimbrel ($42 million for four years), starting pitcher Julio Teheran (six years, $32.4 million), and shortstop Andrelton Simmons (seven years, $58 million) were all locked up for the long-term—along with Heyward's arbitration years being bought out for $13.3 million—and as Wren addressed the collective media, he alluded to the Braves not being done.

"We're really happy with the progress we have made in putting this team together and keeping it together for the long term," he said. "But I wouldn't characterize that we are done. I would characterize it that it's a work in progress."

But at the core of this movement were maneuvers that seemed very much like something Hart would do.

Frankly, it's because he helped guide those signings.

In 1991 when he took over as the Indians' general manager, Hart sought to build his small-market team through trades, the draft, and international scouting. But he also wanted to avoid what happened to the Pirates, who watched Barry Bonds and Bobby Bonilla leave for bigger contracts and bigger markets via free agency.

So Hart inked Sandy Alomar Jr. and Carlos Baerga to extensions that would go into their arbitration years, and followed with similar deals for Albert Belle, Manny Ramirez, Jim Thome, and Omar Vizquel.

He faced criticism from his peers, including a phone call from Dodgers GM Fred Claire that he recalled to *Baseball Prospectus* in 2014.

"John, it's your first full year on the job. What are you thinking?" Claire would say. "John, you have this time, that's what the arbitration process is for—that you can get your arms more around your players."

"Fred," Hart replied, "I understand what you're saying. Believe me, I respect this call. And if I were in L.A. maybe I wouldn't have. You've got to have something pushing you to do it. I've got to be more creative within what we're doing."

Hart's Indians would win six American League Central titles in his ten seasons, including five straight from 1995 to 1999. They reached the World Series twice, including losing to the Braves in six games in 1995.

"We were the smallest of markets and we did it the old-fashioned way," Hart said. "We scouted well, we traded well, we provided opportunity for young players for a number of years and built it and had a great run of about eight years. That's hard to do in a market the size of Cleveland at that time, for sure."

The Braves don't have the same market constraints the Indians do, but it was Hart's tactics that were put into effect in the long-term extensions.

Freeman's deal ran through his first five years of free agency and Simmons was locked up through two, while Kimbrel's could get the Braves one year if they picked up a club option and they held an option for up to two years on Teheran.

The Braves had planned to pursue extensions with all before Hart came aboard, but he would sit in on the meetings—the man who started the trend lending his input.

"He's a great asset for us to have in-house," Wren said after the deals were announced.

Which brings us back to that 2014 press conference and another philosophical approach.

After discussing Wren's ousting, the team that would lead the Braves through the GM transition—Cox, Hart, and Schuerholz himself—and making multiple references to the Braves Way, the franchise's president was asked by a local reporter to define it.

Schuerholz didn't miss a beat.

"It's a special way of identifying young players who you want to become part of your organization with great comfort and expectation that when they put on a Braves uniform, they'll be taught well, instructed well," he said. "Their makeup and their character will allow them to turn into winning championship-caliber players.

"They'll fill the pipeline of this organization with highly capable, high-character, young, winning men who help you win many, many championships on a major-league level, year after year after year."

His response came in rapid-fire fashion, the culture of an organization spelled out in a passionate delivery. If it seemed rehearsed, well, it's a credo he's been adhering to for nearly fifty years.

When the school teacher Schuerholz wrote his letter to Orioles owner Jerold Hoffberger in 1966, his timing couldn't have been better.

The team was going through organizational changes, with Frank Cashen moving to team president, Harry Dalton becoming the new GM, and Lou Gorman becoming director of player development.

That left an opening at the bottom of the baseball operations chart in the form of an assistant director of player development.

Cashen, a former Baltimore sportswriter, knew the Schuerholzes. William "Pop" Schuerholz, John's grandfather, was Loyola College's basketball coach, his father John was a star athlete in Baltimore in the 1930s, and his uncle Donald was a former team captain at Maryland.

Schuerholz interviewed, meeting Cashen, Dalton, and Gorman, and began a period in which he learned with a franchise built on being smart and efficient. The focus was on people, including executives, scouts, and instructors at every level.

It was the Orioles Way.

"I was immersed in an organization that lived it, breathed it, exceeded with it every year," Schuerholz said.

"And then you saw all the work these people did and you were around all these people talking about scouting and player development and sustaining major-league excellence.

"My goodness. If you don't learn in that environment and it doesn't impact you and, really . . . imagine sort of cutting your teeth and forming who you are as a baseball executive amidst that environment."

When Gorman left two years later to become farm director for the expansion Royals, he took Schuerholz and the Orioles Way with him.

"That's where I learned it and then Lou and I both went to Kansas City," Schuerholz said, "and we continued that there and we created some of our own spinoffs of that in Kansas City, and when I came here I brought the same philosophies here."

Like they did in Baltimore and Kansas City—and like he would do later in Atlanta—individuals would be empowered. They would get a clear vision of the organization's expectations and their part in it all. They would be trusted and motivated.

"It's not about the general manager. It's not about the president," Schuerholz said. "It's about the group of people working together . . . this is an administrative team and if you're going to be best at this, not one individual is going to decree or declare or determine how things are going to go.

"You have to set goals and visions, but then you hire the kind of people that have the kind of background that I enjoyed."

The Orioles Way became the Royals Way, and it was then, one early spring training in which he was driving around general manager Jack McKeon, that Schuerholz wrote a poem.

He'll often recite it, a summation of his take on the Way, no matter the franchise.

"I" and "my" are words oft used by those who them-
selves are confused. Why won't their super egos trust the
use of words like "we" and "us"?

The man seated next to Schuerholz as he offered that
definition of the Braves Way understood because he shares
the same views.

Hart was an Expos minor leaguer—as was Wren—
for three years, but after hitting .233 over three seasons he
went back to his native Florida to go to school.

Eleven years after playing his final game, Hart broke
into coaching in 1982 with the Orioles. He would spend sev-
en seasons with stops in the Appalachian, Carolina, Southern, and International Leagues, and was Baltimore's third-
base coach. But a call from newly appointed Indians GM
Hank Peters, who wanted to groom Hart to be his replacement, pulled him out of the dugout and into the front office.

He was schooled in the same way of transforming a
franchise as Schuerholz, creating a friendship between them
as rival GMs and, later, both part of the Braves brain trust.

"He started with Baltimore; I started with Baltimore,"
Hart said. "It's different, I was a field guy and spent the
first half of my career on the field—different ways to get
to the front office—but I think philosophically there's a lot
of similarities I think in the philosophy on what and how
you build an organization.

"[I] watched how he did it, he watched how I did it.
We did it a little differently: he had great pitching, I had
great offense."

After the 2001 season Hart left Cleveland for Texas,
and in July 2004 he was given an extension that guaranteed
two more years, but also included a stipulation that after it
was terminated it would add five more years with Hart as
senior advisor.

As that deal wound down Hart was also working as an
analyst for MLB Network and weighed his options.

"I had a lot of opportunities when I stepped down in Texas to go back in and do the same thing with clubs," Hart said.

On hand as advisor, Hart was the logical choice to succeed Wren, but when asked point-blank if the interim GM would seek the position full-time, he replied, "It's a little early in the game to begin thinking that far ahead."

Schuerholz, though, had other ideas.

"We have not completely closed or opened that door," he shot in. "That's what he meant to say."

That door would, in fact, open.

Throughout the transition team's meetings, Hart would pull out his list of candidates and ask the group, "Okay, are we going to talk about the GMs?" Schuerholz would get up, take a phone call, or leave to go to the bathroom.

Hart got the point.

"I think all along I did feel and know that John clearly wanted me to take this job," he said.

While Schuerholz was back in Kansas City for Game One of the 2014 World Series, he attended a cocktail party with members of MLB Commissioner Bud Selig's office. Owners and other baseball executives were in attendance, and one topic came up over and over again.

"Why don't you talk John Hart into taking a job with the Braves?" Schuerholz was told. "It would be great for you and especially great for the industry to have him back."

Schuerholz returned to Atlanta, and after working on him for weeks, made his final pitch to Hart.

He got his man.

Hart wouldn't be a GM again, though, taking Schuerholz up on his offer, and headed up the efforts to recapture the Braves Way in the newly created position of president of baseball operations. At his side would be John Coppolella, the 36-year-old highly regarded assistant GM, who would be groomed to take over the position (though that wait was shorter than many projected).

"[Hart is] president of baseball operations, and he's going to rule with a velvet glove and an iron hand," a smiling Schuerholz said. "And that's how he is. And be very persuasive. He's got great leadership, personality, people respond to him very well. I've seen it already, I've seen it in the past. He's the best guy to be in this job. It was my best negotiations of my entire baseball career."

Said Hart, 66, of his decision to go all-in once again, "We were able to create something that allowed me to, if you will, not have to wear this thing 24/7, 365. That was the only way I was going to make the full commitment to come back in. . . . They were looking for, if you will, someone that could do the heavy lifting that had the experience before, that shared philosophical similarities."

Hart went to remaking the scouting department, replacing scouting director Tony DeMacio with crosschecker Brian Bridges and making Gordon Blakeley—the former Yankees farm and scouting director—and Roy Clark special assistants to the GM.

Clark had been Atlanta's scouting director from 2000 to 2009—in that span the Braves had produced major leaguers like Yunel Escobar, Freeman, Heyward, Kimbrel, Brian McCann, Kris Medlen, and Mike Minor—before following team president Stan Kasten when he joined the Nationals.

Blakeley had made a major impact in international scouting in New York, signing Robinson Cano, Jose Contreras, Orlando "El Duque" Hernandez, and Hideki Irabu, but it was a place where the Braves had taken a step back. While they had Julio Teheran, the pipeline that delivered Andruw Jones, Rafael Furcal, and Martin Prado wasn't bringing forth impact players like it once was.

"We have to build our farm system back strongly and you do that through scouting, good scouting, Latin American work with scouting," Schuerholz said.

It was also going to take altering the landscape of the immediate future, a task Hart also wasted little time in beginning.

When Hart took the job, he gave the rest of the Braves' powers-that-be his recommendations, dissecting what it would take to be competitive in 2015 and the problems that could pose for '16 and beyond.

"The decision was made from above that deliberately we wanted to reset where we are and they wanted me to do the heavy lifting and that's what I'm doing," Hart said.

The first domino fell a week before Thanksgiving, as Heyward—the Gold Glove–winning right fielder and a product of metro Atlanta's famed East Cobb Baseball program—was dealt to the Cardinals for Shelby Miller and pitching prospect Tyrell Jenkins. Heyward's spot in right field would go to Nick Markakis, a multi-time Gold Glove winner himself, who in December inked a four-year, $44 million deal.

Hart wasn't done dealing, though, receiving hauls of prospects as he dealt Justin Upton to the Padres in December and catcher/outfielder Evan Gattis to the Astros in January. Then, a day before the 2015 season began, the Braves stunningly traded Kimbrel and B. J. Upton—who was now going by his given name, Melvin Jr.—to San Diego in a deal that included more vaunted minor leaguers. The Padres would also be absorbing all of the $46.35 million remaining on Upton's contract.

"As we began to, if you will, reset this club, I think it was a bold move," Hart said. "It was a well-thought-out move, it was a much-deliberated move as to, 'do we take one more run in 2015 knowing that we're going to need to sign three free-agent starters, because the system is not ready yet?'

"We don't have the starting pitching and are we going to hold guys for one year as we go forward? If you sign those guys you have no chance to get your two corner guys [Justin Upton and Jason Heyward] and then you compact that with the fact that this club had some bad contracts. That was a big key."

The flurry of moves had the Braves' farm system suddenly number two in the rankings of ESPN.com's Keith Law, with ten of their top sixteen prospects coming via those trades, which continued into the 2015 season in deals that saw Alex Wood and Chris Johnson leave Atlanta.

"At the end of it there was enormous flexibility it gives us going forward and we were able to move out from some contracts that weren't working for us," Hart said. "It was a lot of pieces and a lot of young players coming back."

It was about creating that flexibility and restocking the lower levels, two initiatives that went hand-in-hand for positioning the Braves to be a force again, and while Hart was the face of the movement, it was Coppolella that did much of the heavy lifting.

He was rewarded for those efforts, as the Notre Dame product, who worked his way up from a Yankees intern and was lauded for his ability to utilize advanced statistics, was named GM on October 1, 2015.

Then 37, he was the youngest GM in baseball. That it came after a 95-loss season, the Braves' worst since 1990's 97 losses, which carried its parallels, as Atlanta followed that year by hiring the game's most junior GM in Schuerholz.

"When John Schuerholz took over as GM here twenty-five years ago, we won fourteen straight [division] titles," Coppolella said at his press conference. "And it's been nearly ten years since he has been out of the GM chair and we've won only one [division] title. What we need to do is get back to young, winning, upside players. We took the first step toward that this year."

He wasted little time in making perhaps his riskiest move, sending Simmons, a winner of two Gold Gloves and a Platinum Glove as the NL's best overall defender—but whose bat never caught up to his all-world fielding—to the Angels in a five-player deal. In return, Atlanta received Anaheim's top-ranked prospect in left-handed pitcher Sean Newcomb, and also righty Chris Ellis, another highly touted arm.

In shipping off a fan favorite and arguably the game's best defensive player, Coppolella understood how it would be perceived. But he was unabashed in defending what he deemed a deal so good the Braves couldn't pass it up, even if it was a stunner for his first major deal.

"If you want to start it out with a big trade, as it worked out that way for me . . . I'm fine with that baptism by fire," he said the night of the move.

It was an aggressive start to Coppolella's tenure, and one he followed up at his first MLB Winter Meetings, dealing Miller to the Diamondbacks for a package that—like in the Simmons deal—not only helped the team in the immediate future by adding outfielder Ender Inciarte, but also brought them shortstop Dansby Swanson, the number-one pick in the 2015 draft, and right-hander Aaron Blair, Arizona's top pick in 2013.

"We added to what we've been trying to do for the last year," Hart said. "We stayed very true over the past twelve months to what we said during the Jason Heyward trade announcement, the first real trade we made here. That we were going to try to stay true to walk parallel paths: to try to win and stay competitive, but try to build something that is going to be long and lasting. The Braves Way. We are going to revamp the farm system."

And they're doing it with a sense of urgency, because if there's one narrative that's fueling all things Braves, it's that 2017 and SunTrust Park are looming.

"We know '17 is sitting out there big," Hart said.

Centennial Olympic Stadium, built just south of Atlanta–Fulton County Stadium, was the main attraction of the 1996 Summer Games.

It was the site of Muhammad Ali—his arm shaking from Parkinson's disease—serving as the surprise lighter of the Olympic torch; it was where Carl Lewis would win his fourth consecutive long jump; and beginning with Opening Day 1997, it was retrofitted as the "Home of the Braves," as nearby Atlanta–Fulton County Stadium was imploded.

But less than twenty years later, and with the stadium—which is owned by the Atlanta–Fulton County Recreation Authority—needing expensive upgrades, the franchise announced it was on the move, leaving behind downtown Atlanta for a spot at the intersection of I-75 and I-285 in suburban Cobb County.

"Turner Field, which we do not own, is in need of hundreds of millions of dollars of upgrades," Schuerholz said in a statement when the move was announced in November 2013. "Unfortunately, that massive investment would not do anything to improve access or the fan experience. These are issues we simply cannot overcome.

"This decision to move was not easy, and we have mixed emotions about leaving a ballpark that holds so many great memories. However, knowing that our lease will expire in 2016, we have devoted our time trying to secure the best option for our fans, our team, and our organization. We believe this new site will be the best location for our fans and our organization for the next thirty years."

They'll move into a new mixed-use development for the start of the 2017 season that includes the 41,500-seat SunTrust Park (down 8,596 from Turner Field), a

50,000-square foot entertainment venue, and nearly a million square feet of restaurant, residential, hotel, and office space.

Atlanta mayor Kasim Reed issued a response, saying in part, "The Atlanta Braves are one of the best baseball teams in America, and I wish them well. We have been working very hard with the Braves for a long time, and at the end of the day, there was simply no way the team was going to stay in downtown Atlanta without city taxpayers spending hundreds of millions of dollars to make that happen."

A 365-day-a-year destination is the Braves' goal, but it's ultimately about the product on the field, and they will enter their new home hoping plenty of the pieces added by those sweeping changes of Hart's first year on the job and the early work of Coppolella fill the roster.

"Draft well, develop well, and have, if you will, a core of young players coming that can either help you when they walk through the doors at SunTrust or be, if you will, enough ammunition if you have to go make a trade, you've got pieces you can trade," Hart said.

That in itself, is the Braves Way. It's scouting players, developing them, and flipping organizational depth into major-league assets, a mission that would seem to be the motive of any franchise. But Schuerholz stresses you need the right people, and he believes they're now in place.

"You have to have an organization that subjugates the 'I and my'—my poem—to 'We and us' and if you have the 'We and us' attitude, you're going to succeed if you have good, strong, dedicated people," he said. "That's what we have now."

The Braves Way is set in the front office, but on the field it becomes something different.

Mark Lemke is a product of it. Overachievement in the form of a 27th-round pick, he rose up and became a key piece in the 1990s run, playing in 1,038 games over ten years. To him, the philosophy boiled down to one word: Pride.

"It's the way you play the game," he said. "You play the game the right way. You play fundamentally sound, you respect the uniform, you respect the name on the front of your jersey on and off the field. You have character in the clubhouse, when you're outside the stadium, when you interact with fans, your neighbors, regardless of what it is."

It's a sentiment that was shared by the player that Lemke believes personifies the Braves Way: Hall of Fame left-hander Tom Glavine.

"It was just that pride in what we were, what we did, and the brand that we were trying to represent," he said.

Current Braves manager Fredi Gonzalez and Hart shared a conversation about effort. A team can be five games under .500, but it's how they play the game that decides how fans leave the stadium thinking about those players.

"Usually the team that goes out does it the right way, they give you the hustle," Gonzalez said. "The fans say 'Man, these guys lost today, but they battled.' Instead of 'I wonder how much they care?'—and it's the same record, but two different teams and two different perceptions."

To a man, that's what the Braves' brass believe they had under Cox and Schuerholz and it's what they're trying to regain with a regime led first by Hart and now Coppolella.

"I feel like we made a dynamic decision to make a change to go in a new direction—or actually a new, old direction, just go back to what we were—it works," Schuerholz said. "I've seen it work in Baltimore, I've seen it work in Kansas City, I've seen it work here, and now it's working again."

The Hall Calls Once Again

John Smoltz had two warnings for reporters the day before his Hall of Fame speech.

For the first time in his life, he would say, he was going to read a speech. "I think it's the easiest, safest way to stay on course, because I've always passionately spoke about what I've known and people appreciate that, but I can take some rabbit [holes]."

Secondly—and maybe most importantly, based on what people would remember from his time at the podium—he had something special in store for his Hall of Fame teammate Greg Maddux.

"It's probably the best part of my speech," he said. "I can't wait. I have a trick up my sleeve for Maddux. I'm hoping that I can pull that off flawlessly."

Smoltz took the stage, joining Craig Biggio, Randy Johnson, and Pedro Martinez in the Class of 2015, and the right-hander launched into a twenty-nine-minute opus.

He name-dropped good friend Jeff Foxworthy, dug into his past as an accordion player—at four, he was playing polka parties—and somehow, as he would admit later, inadvertently omitted former Braves owner Ted Turner.

But midway through his speech, he would have his answer for his former rotation mates.

The only pitcher in history with at least 200 wins and 150 saves became the first to add a follicle prop to his speech, as he broke out a long, black wig that seemed more fitting for a metal revival band than Cooperstown.

"(Tom Glavine), Maddux, back when I had hair, we had the time of our lives," Smoltz said as he donned the faux mane. "It's the only time, Greg, you're not going to be able to talk about my bald head."

But Smoltz wasn't content with just being a good sport in response to the 2014 ceremony, in which Maddux mentioned "watching John Smoltz's hairline recede."

"Recently, I lost twenty pounds," Smoltz said, "and they helped me find it. Thank you, guys."

Humor has always been part of Smoltz's makeup, but so too is his passion for the game. It came as no surprise that the man who would, in his second career, become an analyst for MLB Network, used the HOF platform to combat "an epidemic, something affecting our game."

Growing up playing baseball and basketball in Lansing, Michigan, Smoltz drew a loud applause as he said, "Baseball is not a year-round sport. You have an opportunity to be athletic and play other sports."

In the days, weeks and months leading up to his induction ceremony, Smoltz spoke out about the rash of Tommy John surgeries, known to doctors as ulnar collateral ligament reconstructions, in the game. It was by calling out America's parents while he had the baseball world's attention that he hoped to help bring an end to the rash of young pitchers undergoing the surgery.

"I want to encourage you, if nothing else, know that your children's desire and passion to play baseball is something they can do without a competitive pitch," Smoltz said. "Every throw a kid makes today is a competitive pitch. They don't go outside, they don't throw enough. They're competing and maxing out too hard too early."

Ulnar collateral ligament reconstruction and the process of coming back from it have become the norm in baseball. But when Smoltz was returning from the surgery in 2001, he had his doubts.

At 34, post-surgery, he made five starts with a combined 5.76 ERA, including an outing against the Rockies in which he gave up five runs on six hits in just three innings.

"I was going to retire," Smoltz said.

Then came one of what Smoltz would call the four most important phone calls in his life.

The first was from the Tigers when he was drafted, the hometown kid joining the team he rooted for. Next, came the news that he had been traded to the Braves in 1987. Much later he'd receive the word that he'd joined the game's most iconic names in Cooperstown.

But in between that trade and the HOF came the conversation that would help to salvage Smoltz's career.

It was Tommy John himself.

The surgery's first recipient, via the work of Dr. Frank Jobe in 1974 when he was 34, John had heard Smoltz was contemplating ending his career.

"John, I'm telling you, don't do it," John told him. "You've got a lot of career left. I pitched eleven years afterward."

Said Smoltz as he thinks back on that talk, "I just . . . no one that I knew had had it at the age of thirty-four until I heard that he had the same surgery at the same age and he pitched eleven more years. Now granted, he wasn't a flame-thrower, but it was like a much-needed phone call to get me over the top."

Admittedly, the power pitcher has never thought too highly of himself. He recalled going into the Detroit Pistons locker room while at the height of his career. He couldn't believe the likes of Joe Dumars knew his name.

But Smoltz is all too aware that his legacy is intertwined with the surgery. He would go on to save 154 games after having it—becoming a three-time All-Star closer along the way—and then returning to the rotation with two more All-Star nods. As he stood on that stage with a collection of the game's greats behind him, he did so as the first player to undergo that procedure and reach the HOF.

"I believe the trend that we are going today, I could be the very last that ever makes the Hall of Fame with Tommy John," he said. "If it continues to—at the rate that it's going, the injuries, I don't see us getting any better until we figure out ways that, you know, we can stop these injuries from happening at too early of an age."

That remains to be seen, and it may ultimately force voters to reevaluate the numbers that are seen as a pitcher's passport to the Hall. But the great ones find a way to adjust to whatever era they're dealing with, just as Smoltz, Glavine, and Maddux did while pitching in the steroid era.

"I think that's kind of the criteria for pretty much all of the Hall of Famers that are in there right now," he said. "That's what makes them so great."

Fifteen members of the Hall of Fame forged their legacies as Braves, from Hugh Duffy in Boston to Warren Spahn in Milwaukee and Smoltz and his cohorts in Atlanta. What's certain, though, is that Smoltz won't be the last.

Chipper Jones is likely to follow as a first-ballot selection in 2018, and former general manager and current team president John Schuerholz could make it too.

Unlike his rotation mate Maddux, Smoltz was careful not to add fuel to the fire for Jones.

"To Chipper Jones, soon to be inducted in the Hall of Fame, another one of the Atlanta Braves," Smoltz said. "I'm not going to say anything about him because he'll have the mic last."

But he couldn't resist taking at least a subtle dig at the third baseman, who has been known to speak his mind on social media.

"Would somebody please steal his Twitter account?" Smoltz said, laughing.